THE HISTORICAL JESUS: CARPENTER FROM NAZARETH? OR NAZARENE HIGH PRIEST?

OTHER BOOKS BY P.J. GOTT AND LOGAN LICHT

Following Philo in Search of The Magdalene, The Virgin, The Men Called Jesus, published in 2015

Following Philo from Ba'al and Asherah to Jesus and Mary Magdalene, published in 2018.

THE HISTORICAL JESUS

Carpenter from Nazareth?

or

Nazarene High Priest?

P.J. Gott and Logan Licht

Quiet Waters Publications
2025

Copyright ©2025 by P.J. Gott. All rights reserved. Printed in the United States of America. No part of this book may be used or reproduced in any manner whatsoever without written permission except in the case of brief quotations embodied in critical articles and reviews.

Quiet Waters Publications

http://www.quietwaterspub.com

ISBN 978-1-962698-10-8

Dedication

To my beloved granddaughter

Amanda,

May your brilliant and beautiful Goddess Energy light The Way to the love and compassion The Nazarenes delivered to the people of the Roman Empire.

And may Goddess Light dissipate the cloud of ignorance that manifests as hate and greed.

"Is not this the carpenter,
the son of Mary, and brother of
James, and Joseph, and Judas, and Simon?"
Mark 6:3

***

"We have…found this man…
a ringleader of the
heresy of the Nazarenes."
Acts 24:5

***

Paul testified:
"But this I admit to you,
that according to *The Way*,
which they call a heresy,
I worship the Elohim of our ancestors…"
Acts 24:14

***

Jesus said
"…'To you has been given
the secret of the Kingdom of Elohim,
but for those outside, everything is in *enigmas*,
so that they may indeed see but not perceive,
and may indeed hear, but not understand…'"
Mark 4:10

Author's Note

My search for *The Historical Jesus* was set in motion in October 1999 when I was approached by a man near the Church of Saint Francis of Assisi in Rancho de Toas, New Mexico.

This bearded, disheveled panhandler explained that a psychiatrist sentenced him to a life of poverty and despair with a misdiagnosis of *Messianic Ideation*. He assured me he was not crazy. This encounter piqued my obsessive-compulsive curiosity, and I just let it carry me away.

My first step in 2000 was to order books published by the *Jesus Seminar*; ten years later a member of that group, Dr. Charles Hedrick,[1] taught a series of classes at the church I attended. His expertise: Christian origins and the Gospels of *Mark* and *Thomas*.

A year or so later, a prominent German-American scholar, Dr. David Trobisch,[2] taught a series of classes at the same church. His areas of expertise: Christian origins, ancient New Testament manuscripts, Paul's epistles, and Marcionite Christianity.

I asked Dr. Trobisch to look at some of my "discoveries," and I asked him to critique my methodology and my writing skills—or lack thereof.

He warned that I would receive harsh criticism from orthodox scholars, and he challenged me to defend each of my claims with evidence that satisfied him.

Gott

Chapter One

Jesus: History or Myth?

The debate over *Jesus, fact or fiction,* has produced millions of pages of research notes, an infinite number of scholarly opinions and articles, and thousands of books.

But no consensus.

Over the centuries, an assortment of "scholarly methods" have been proposed, tested, accepted, revised then rejected.

And still the question remains.

The current popular method, *Historical Criticism,*[3] investigates the origins of ancient texts to understand "the world behind the text"[4] and emphasizes a process that "delays any assessment of scripture's truth and relevance until after the act of interpretation has been carried out."[5]

The historical-critical method assumes objective reality and an objective meaning embedded within a text that can be extracted by a skillful interpreter.

The historical-critical method, like the scientific method, begins with a hypothesis, tests it by applying the method to what is being studied, and either accepts the initial hypothesis, revises it, or abandons it.[6]

Most searches for the historical Jesus follow a similar path of collecting, examining, and testing evidence pulled from New Testament texts, the writings of early church apologists, people and events reported by ancient historians, and scholarly research over time.

But all searches have faced a major but unrecognized obstacle: the *Apostle Paul* and his supporters conspired to perpetrate a massive fraud that guarantees conventional sources and established methods will never lead to *The Historical Jesus.*

These roadblocks have been reinforced throughout the centuries by universally accepted "rules" that discourage explorations outside established scholars' defined boxes. The ridicule for doing so is merciless.

So it may seem unlikely that an ancient, unorthodox method that has been repeatedly rejected by historians and biblical scholars might lead to a candidate that qualifies, beyond a reasonable doubt, as *The Historical Jesus.*

Chapter Two

Nazareth vs Nazarene

The evidence that leads to *The Historical Jesus* is from the same sources that have previously failed to answer the question definitively. This is the nature, the beauty, and the genius of enigmas.

Matthew 2:23 is the first major hurdle to finding the historical Jesus:

> "...and he went and lived in a town called Nazareth. So was fulfilled what was said through the prophets, that he would be called a Nazarene."

Mark 1:9 concurs:

> "Jesus came from Nazareth in Galilee..."

When Rome united church and state under Nicene Christianity, no one worked harder than Epiphanius, Bishop of Salamis (c. 320–403), to separate Jesus from the Nazarene sect and to discount all the NZR and NSR heresies that people were apparently associating with "The Nazarene."

Epiphanius wrote *Panarion* c. 375 in an attempt to dispel any suspicion that "Jesus the Nazarene" might be associated with the *Nasaraean* or *Nazarene* sect or the *Nazirites* of Moses. His efforts suggest the Church had cause to be concerned and assigned him to address it.

In his attempt to discount the Nazarenes, Epiphanius reveals important information about them. He first addresses the group he identifies as "Nasaraeans," writing:

> The Nasaraeans...were Jews by nationality...They acknowledged Moses and believed that he had received laws—*not this law, however, but some other*. And so, they were Jews who kept all the Jewish observances, but they *would not offer sacrifice or eat meat*. They considered it unlawful to eat meat or make sacrifices with it. *They claim that these Books are fictions, and that none of these customs were instituted by the fathers.* This was the difference between the Nasaraeans and the others.

It is notable that the Nasaraeans rejected animal sacrifice—aka, *vicarious atonement*—and they were vegetarians.

Epiphanius continues,

> Nasaraeans, meaning, "rebels," who forbid all flesh eating, and do not eat living things at all. They have the holy names of patriarchs which are in the Pentateuch, up through Moses and Joshua the son of Nun, and they believe in them—I mean Abraham, Isaac, Jacob, and the earliest ones, and Moses himself, and Aaron, and Joshua. But they hold that *the scriptures of the Pentateuch were not written by Moses, and maintain that they have others.*[7]

Who could possibly question these authorities' claims that "Jesus the Nazarene" was **NOT** to be confused with the heretical Nazarenes? He was called *The Nazarene* only because he spent time in Nazareth! He was "Jesus *OF* Nazareth!"

Here's the problem: Abundant evidence reveals that *Nazareth* has nothing to do with Jesus being called *The Nazarene*. The historical Jesus is yet to be found because

"Jesus from Nazareth" is *not* a historical person and can *never* be found.

The Trinitarian God-man from Nazareth is a fictional creation by a devout Judean willing to make a few minor compromises in order to preserve the superiority of the misogynistic YHWH. The blood of Jesus replaced the blood of a lamb; YHWH no longer required circumcision. The search for a "historical" Jesus from Nazareth nailed to a cross was *designed* to fail.

Chapter Three

Elijah's Miracle

The successful search for *The Historical Jesus* begins with the Nazarenes at Mount Carmel, the location of one of the most important events in Judaism.

According to Hebrew Bible stories, the popularity of the Israelites' *Ba'el and Asherah* persisted for generations and, time after time, sparked bloody conflicts. The story of Elijah's victory at Mount Carmel reveals the tactics one side employed to win converts.

The King James Version of the contest is remarkable for what it omits:

> "Now therefore send, and gather to me all Israel unto mount Carmel, and the prophets of Baal four hundred and fifty, and <u>the prophets of the groves</u> four hundred, which eat at Jezabel's table" (1 Kings 18:19).

King James authors were so fearful of naming a goddess that they translate the word *Asherah* as "the groves,"[8] leaving the die-hard King-James devotees ignorant of Asherah's relationship to Judaism.

Asherah was a goddess in the ancient Near East who was associated with fertility, motherhood, and the sea. Eloah, later *Ba'eL* or *aB'eL,* translated "Father Eloah," was her consort. She was revered among the Canaanites; Asherah poles in Israelite worship sites represented a blending of Canaanite and Israelite religious practices. However,

Asherah was rejected and strictly forbidden by YHWH's Kings.

Elijah accuses *Ahab*, King of Israel, of forsaking YHWH's *Commandments* and following Ba'eL and Asherah. Kings and Queens adopted the names, *YHWH, Ba'eL* and *Asherah*, or variations, in order to claim the unquestionable authority of their envisioned Creator. The name *Ah-aB* claims *Ba'eL* as this King's "brother."[9]

Yawists proposed that an all-powerful *YHWH* created all things in the universe alone; masculine energy is all that is needed to produce life on Earth.

Elohists proposed that an invisible, all-powerful *eLoHiM* —*Ba'eL and Asherah*—created all things in the universe, masculine and feminine energy—positive-negative forces bound together by a neutral center to produce life on Earth.

YHWH's Kings are depicted as strict authoritarians enforcing YHWH's hard and fast *Commandments* with harsh consequences, but with sins forgiven through faith in a sacrificial lamb.

Elohim's King and Queen are portrayed as benevolent "Father-Mother," offering suggestions and guidance but willing to consider mistakes as "learning experiences" that carry their own consequences. As Epiphanius notes, "they would not offer sacrifice."

Elijah invites the Israelites to gather at Mount Carmel, specifically, the "prophets of Ba'eL" and the "prophets of Asherah."[10] Elijah addresses the gathered Israelites and prophets:

"How long will you hesitate between two opinions? If YHWH is the Elohim, follow Him; but if Ba'eL is the Elohim, follow Him."

So Elijah devises a test to prove to the Israelites that they would be safer and more prosperous with YHWH as their deity. All agree that the deity who responds to the prophets' petitions to ignite wood will be declared the one and only, *God*.

The prophets of Ba'eL and Asherah go first, carefully stacking wood on the altar then fervently praying to Ba'eL and Asherah to ignite a fire. Nothing happens.

Elijah stacks wood on the altar; then he builds a trench around it and pours water into the trench. Only then does he call for prayer to ask YHWH to send fire.

> ...the fire of YHWH fell, and consumed the burnt offering and the wood...When all the people saw it, they fell on their faces; and they said, 'YHWH, He is Elohim,' YHWH, He is Elohim." Then Elijah said to them, 'Seize the prophets of Ba'eL; do not let one of them escape. So they seized them; and Elijah brought them down to the brook Kishon, and slew them there'" (1 Kings 18:38-40).

Unfortunately, the prophets of Ba'eL and Asherah were not given the opportunity to explain that sulfur and quicklime ignite when combined with water. This chemical reaction was well known within elite circles during Elijah's time.

The naïve Israelites abandoned their King and Queen because they believed chemically-produced, spontaneous combustion was a message from YHWH that proved him to be the one and only *God*.

Elijah's deception paid off as *Big Lies* often do.

But Israel's Queen Jezebel[11] was aware of the natural law behind the "miracle" that deceived her people. Elijah, fearing retribution for the slaughter of her prophets, flees. The conflicts between the prophets of YHWH and the prophets of Ba'eL and Asherah continue until King Nebuchadnezzar intervenes.

It was Queen Jezebel who introduced Ba'eL and Asherah to the Israelites; she is eventually slaughtered (2 Kings 9:30-

37) and became the Christian archetype of the wicked woman.

The prophets of Ba'eL and Asherah who survived Elijah's ethnic cleansing on Mount Carmel remained faithful to the Elohim, and they remained on their sacred mountain. Thereafter, persecuted Nazarenes were forced to worship in secret places, either the top of mountains or underground.

The Kings of YHWH slaughtered those who refused to bow down to their all-powerful male deity. The Kings and Queens of Elohim were pacifists who taught that love and peace are superior to hate and conflict.

One of the Nazarene "Secret Places" was discovered in 1917 beneath the Porta Maggiore and the Baker's Tomb on the east side of Rome. Unfortunately, for some reason, it is no longer open to the public.

"The basilica has been interpreted as a place of worship or funerary building.

"Beyond the hypotheses on its function, the elegant decorations make this basilica a work of art dating back to the beginning of the I century AD."

Photo Credits: Soprintendenza Speciale di Roma –Archeologia Belle Arti Paesaggio[12]

Chapter Four

Allegory vs Enigma

Fast forward from Mount Carmel to the destruction of Jerusalem's first temple when King Nebuchadnezzar transported Judean priests and scribes to Babylon for reeducation and indoctrination.

The Babylonians exerted total control over Jewish leadership for more than sixty years, from c. 600 to c. 539 BCE when Babylonian King Cyrus began allowing some priests and their families to return to Jerusalem. The Book of Ezra dates the construction of the Second Temple to 537 BCE.

Virtually ignored is a tidbit of information which appears to be irrelevant to *Historical Jesus* research. Neoplatonist biographer Iamblichus (c. 245–c. 325 CE)[13] provides most of what is known about the Greek philosopher and polyhistor, Pythagoras.

Iamblichus reports that Pythagoras (c. 570–c. 495 BCE) met with the Nazarenes at Mount Carmel before traveling to Egypt where he conducted "most studious research" and "acquired wisdom" from Egyptian priests. He was permitted to observe mystery rituals, and he studied Egyptian astronomy and geometry. After twenty-two years of travel he was taken to *Babylon* where "the Magi instructed him in their venerable knowledge," including arithmetic, music, and "other sciences." Pythagoras remained in Babylon twelve years, where he would have crossed paths with Judean priests and scribes .[14]

First century Jewish philosopher *Philo "the Jew" of Alexandria* (c. 10 BCE–c. 74 CE) was also known as "the Pythagorean"[15] and provides the definition of a *polyhistor*:

> I admire the Lover of Wisdom...collecting and thinking it fit to weave together many things, though different, and proceeding from different sources, into the same web; for taking the first two elements from the grammatical knowledge...reading and writing, and taking from...poets...and ancient history and... arithmetic and geometry...and calculations...and borrowing from music rhyme, and metre, and harmony, and chromatics, and diatonics, and combined and disjoined melodies; and...rhetoric and invention...language, and arrangement, and memory, and action; and from philosophy...all the other things of which human life consists, he has put together in one most admirably arranged work, combining great learning of one kind with great learning of another kind.[16]

Philo alludes to a unique feature of biblical Hebrew when writing of the Essenes in "Every Good Man is Free":

> Then one takes up the holy volume and reads it, and another of the men of the greatest experience comes forward and *explains what is not very intelligible*, for a great many precepts are delivered in *enigmatical modes of expression*, and allegorically, as the old fashion was.[17]

Lucius Mestrius Plutarchus **(c. 46–c. 120 CE) left a most intriguing clue to first-century methods of preserving and transmitting information that an adversary could not alter.**

> Pythagoras greatly admired the Egyptian priests, and, copying their symbolism and secret teachings, *incorporated his doctrines in enigmas.* As a matter of fact, most of the Pythagorean precepts do not at all fall short of the writings that are called hieroglyphs.

> ...Whenever you hear the traditional tales which the Egyptians tell about the gods, their wanderings, dismemberments, and many experiences...you must not think that any of these tales actually happened *in the manner in which they are related.*
>
> If you *listen to the **stories about the gods** in this way*... you may avoid superstition which is no less an evil than atheism.[18]

Like Philo the Pythagorean-Jew before him, Plutarch the Greek historian explains that enigmas are the preferred means of telling stories about the gods. Enigmas are similar to allegories, but the difference, although subtle, is important.

Merriam-Webster defines "allegory" as:

> 1: the expression by means of symbolic fictional figures and actions of truths or generalizations about human existence; also: an instance (as in a story or painting) of such expression; 2: a symbolic representation.

Merriam-Webster defines "enigma" as:

> "1: an obscure speech or writing; 2: something hard to understand or explain; 3: an inscrutable or mysterious person." Synonyms listed include: "mystery"; "puzzle"; "riddle"; "secret."

Thus, the solution to an allegory can be based on an individual's personal life experiences and expectations. It can, therefore, produce a multitude of subjective opinions, but no conclusive solution.

On the other hand, an enigma (mystery; puzzle; riddle; secret) can be solved, but it requires special knowledge or a key. There is but one solution, and it cannot be influenced by an individual's subjective interpretation as long as the key is intact and properly utilized.

When an enigma is put into writing, its creator also provides the clues which solve the mystery, puzzle, or riddle. Only certain people—the initiated—are given the key. With access to this key, virtually anyone can solve the puzzle and reconstruct the secret hidden within the enigma. Most important, all who do so will reach a similar conclusion.

To us, of course, this is a strange method of transmitting factual information. But it was a common practice two thousand years ago as a way to pass the *Losers'* version of events through time invisibly attached to the *Victors'* surviving version.

And it was not confined to religious texts!

Philo's Method is traditionally referred to as the *allegorical interpretation* of scripture; a more accurate definition is *a systematic method of interpreting enigmatical modes of expression imbedded in texts.*

Plutarch associates the method with Pythagoras, who learned it from the Egyptians. This dates the method to at least the 6th century BCE during Pythagoras' lifetime.

Most scholars searching for the historical Jesus have relied on the integrity of early Christian leaders, i.e. Irenaeus, Eusebius, and Jerome, plus the literal interpretations of the Four Gospels, *Acts*, and Paul's letters. And they have accepted the conclusions of previous experts who did the same.

We have not followed in their well-worn path.

Chapter Five

Heresy or History?

"Philo's Method" has never been considered worthy of testing, perhaps because it has long been declared a heresy. Early church father Irenaeus (c. 130-202 CE) described it as a "farce and falsehood."[19]

In 1885 Frederic W. Farrar read from eight earlier lectures by the late Rev. John Bampton (1689-1751) as required by Bampton's Last Will and Testament. In 1886 MacMillan and Company in London published these lectures titled "History of Interpretation."[20]

Bampton criticizes what he called "Philo's Rules,":

"All this 'madness' is reduced to 'method' by a set of rules, half Haggadistic, half Stoic, but entirely inapplicable."

He lists six rules which Bampton considered to be a heretical absurdity.

Between 1901 and 1906, the editors of *The Jewish Encyclopedia* published an article, "Philo Judeaus,"[21] which appears to have unpacked Bampton's six rules, teased out twenty-one, and incorporated them into their commentary. They are similar in content and sequence to the Philo material that originated in Bampton's and Farrar's lectures, and the authors reinforce its uselessness:

> Philo's teaching was not Jewish, but was derived from Greek philosophy. Desiring to convert it into a Jewish doctrine, he applied the Stoic mode of allegoric

interpretation to the Old Testament. No one before Philo, except his now forgotten Alexandrian predecessors, had applied this method to the Old Testament—a method that could produce no lasting results. It was attacked even in Alexandria ("De Vita Mosis," iii. 27 [ii. 168]), and disappeared after the brief florescence of Jewish Hellenism.[22]

No modern researcher has been curious enough—or naïve enough—to investigate this allegedly useless heresy. Philo's Method is simply too far beyond defined limitations to risk the ridicule of colleagues.

Our investigation tests Philo's "heretical" rules that are enumerated in the Jewish Encyclopedia; we apply our tests to Hebrew scripture—and other ancient sources for first century events, i.e., Nicolaus of Damascus, Josephus, Plutarch, Suetonius, Tacitus, Pliny the Younger, et.al.

The Babylonian Talmud[23] reveals the foundation of the Nazarenes' *Project to Preserve*:

> ...with the advent of the
> *House of Hillel*
> and the
> *House of Shammai*,
> the Torah became like two Torahs.[24]

According to the Jerusalem Talmud[25] (Shabbat 1:4:3c), the *House of Shammai* obtained their majority by killing members of the *House of Hillel*, an echo of the slaughter at Mount Carmel and Jezebel, and a precursor of the slaughter of Hypatia at the hands of a gang of Christian zealots in 415,[26] Joan of Arc in 1431, and the Salem Witch Trials of 1692-3—not to mention the Crusades.

"If they won't join you, kill 'em!" Especially if "they" are women.

According to Yevamot 14b, each school kept track of its members' lineages and forbid marriage between the two schools, a reminder and a continuation of the forbidden relationships in *Ezra-Nehemiah*.[27]

The Talmud's "Two Torahs" solves the mystery of the "two versions" of Philo's Essenes described in "Every Good Man is Free": version *one* read by the novice, and version *two* available to those who could solve "enigmatic modes of expression."

These observations are explained by the ingenious feature of *Late Biblical Hebrew* which has been virtually ignored in *orthodox* biblical scholarship.

Late Biblical Hebrew is comprised of only consonants— no vowels, no spaces, no punctuation. These elements are chosen based on the words needed to convey the story being told. This inspired consonant-only script allows a scribe to imbed an occult teaching into a widely-accepted but opposing text. Philo's "experienced Essene" would have known of a "key" which the novice did not have.[28]

Our hypothesis: When Ezra arrived in Jerusalem from Babylon with the Tanakh[29] c. 458 BCE, *Biblical Judaism, Late Biblical Hebrew,* and *Pythagorean instructions for solving enigmas*, arrived with him.

Plutarch suggests it is no coincidence that the *Tanakh* was compiled and edited in Babylon during the time Pythagoras also resided there:

> "Pythagoras greatly admired the Egyptian priests, and, copying their symbolism and secret teachings, *incorporated his doctrines in enigmas.*"

Considering the intersection between Pythagoras and Judean priests in Babylon, it seems reasonable to ask if it's possible that "Pythagoras' doctrines" are secreted within in the Tanakh.

If our hypothesis is correct and enigmas reveal facts hidden within Hebrew scripture and secular history, the doctrines promoted by the *House of Shammai*[30] are revealed in the name *shama*, translated "hear and obey,"[31] i.e., YHWH's *Ten Commandments*.

"Yahweh Shammah"[32] is translated, "Yahweh is there." This school of Jewish instruction would have been devoted to the Yahwist traditions,[33] faith in YHWH ("LORD").

The doctrines promoted by the *House of Hillel* are also revealed in the name: *Hillel* in Biblical Hebrew is HLLL. Rendered *HaLa eL eLa*, the words are translated "Praise God and Goddess."

This school of Essene-Nazarene instruction was devoted to the Elohist traditions, faith in the *Elohim*, "Father-Mother," also known as *Ba'eL and Asherah*, which Elijah discredited and tried to destroy at Mount Carmel.

Hillel is described as a Jewish religious leader, sage and scholar who was associated with the development of the *Mishnah* and the *Talmud*. He came to Israel from Babylon; he was descended from King David; his descendent *Judah ha Nasi* traced his lineage through both the female lineage of the Tribe of Benjamin and the family of King David.[34]

> Hillel lived in Jerusalem during the time of King Herod and the Roman emperor Augustus. In the *Midrash* compilation *Sifre*, the periods of Hillel's life are made parallel to those in the life of Moses. At the age of forty Hillel went to the Land of Israel; forty years he spent in study; and the last third of his life he was the spiritual head of the Jewish people. A biographical sketch can be constructed that Hillel went to Jerusalem in the prime of his life and attained a great age.[35]

According to the *Mishnah*, Hillel went to Jerusalem to study biblical exposition and tradition at the age of 40 in 70 BCE. Born c. 110 BCE, Hillel is same age as Julius Caesar.

The Talmud describes the hardships Hillel overcame before he was admitted to the school of *Sh'maya and Abtalion*.[36] When he settled a question concerning the sacrificial ritual that showed his superiority over the Bnei

Bathyra, the Sanhedrin "Nasi" resigned in favor of Hillel who was thereafter recognized as the highest authority among the Pharisee Jews.

Hillel was the head of the school first associated with *Menahem the Essene*.[37] He is best known, perhaps, as the author of the saying, "That which is hateful to you, do not do unto your fellow. That is the whole Torah; the rest is the explanation; go and learn."[38]

This maxim is parroted in Jesus' instruction, *"Do unto others as you would have them do unto you,"* evidence that Jesus was aware of the doctrines of the *House of Hillel* and incorporated them into his teachings.

The Jewish historian Josephus writes that Hillel's great-grandson, *Simeon ben Gamliel,* belonged to a very celebrated family and that Hillel "devoted himself to studying the Torah while also working as a *woodcutter.*"[39]

According to the Talmud, Hillel's son was *Simeon ben Hillel*, his grandson was *Gamaliel,* and according to Josephus,[40] his great-grandson was called *Iesous ben Gamaliel.*

Nasi Hillel the "woodcutter," aka, "*carpenter*" is an important piece of the historical Jesus puzzle.

Not only did Gamaliel inherit his grandfather's *House of Hillel*, he was called *Nasi* (translated, "prince") and *Rabban* ("our master") as the president of the Great Sanhedrin in Jerusalem.[41]

Philo's method applied to the opening words of Gen 1:1 reveals the significant difference between the doctrines of Shammai and the doctrines of Hillel:

Shammai, Gen 1:1: BRSTBRLHM..., rendered *BaReSiT BaRa eLoHiM*, is *mistranslated*, "In the beginning created **God**..." (the iM suffix denotes the plural, "gods").

Philo's Rule 16 (per Jewish Encyclopedia): "the artificial interpretation of a single expression..." signals that the mistranslation of *eLoHiM* as "god" requires the *initiated* to find another translation.

Hillel, Gen 1:1 BRSTBRLHM... can be *correctly* rendered *BaR* (son of) *iS* ("man") *eT*[42] ("and") *aB oR* ("father light") *eLaH eM* ("god mother"): "Son of Man and Father Light, Goddess Mother," the Nazarene Holy Trinity.

Jesus refers to himself as "The Son of Man" more than eighty times in the New Testament, leaving many to wonder what exactly he meant. The phrase is scattered throughout the Four Gospels, suggesting it may have been a late addition by the "final editor" to prove the relationship between *Jesus the Nazarene* and the *Nazarene Holy Trinity*.

"Son of Man" opens the Nazarene version of the Hebrew Bible to introduce the *Archetypal Family*: a wise, enlightened "Father," a loving, compassionate "Mother," and offspring who inherit the traits of both.

More important, however, this intentional association with the opening words of Genesis serves as *proof* that Jesus the Nazarene rejected YHWH and embraced "Father-Mother."

Shammai's Jews would have rejected any suggestion of a Holy Trinity in which the *Feminine* is placed on the same level as *Son of Man* and *Father God*. Shammai replaced "God-Mother" with "Holy Spirit," and Paul adopted it for his YHWH-serving invention, Christianity.

Many questions that surround Paul and his rejection of "Jesus the Nazarene" are answered in *The Acts of the Apostles*, an attempt—against all odds—to expose Paul's lies and preserve the hidden truth.

David J. Trobisch[43] proposes that *Polycarp, Bishop of Smyrna*, compiled and edited the final edition of the New Testament and assigned coordinating titles to each of the Four Gospels.[44]

According to Eusebius, the Romans burned Polycarp at the stake c. 166-7, allegedly because he refused to burn incense to honor Emperor Marcus Aurelius.⁴⁵ Rome's preferred methods of execution were crucifixion and beheading, and of course food for lions; whereas, the Church's preferred method was burning at the stake.

If Polycarp wrote *The Acts of the Apostles*, and if, as we propose, *Acts* is an enigmatic expose of facts the Early Church was determined to hide, Polycarp would certainly be eligible for a tortuous execution.

Was Polycarp's "heresy" the secrets he exposed in *Acts*? More important, can Polycarp's revelations surrounding Paul and the origins of Christianity be recovered?

Chapter Six

Solving Enigmas in The Acts of the Apostles

The author of *Acts* brings *Jesus the Nazarene* of history back into view when Philo's Method is utilized to solve the enigmas:

> Now, during those days, when the disciples were increasing in number the *Hellenists complained against the Hebrews* because their widows were being neglected in the daily distribution of food (Acts 6:1).

The *Hellenists* were Hillel's *Essene-Nazarenes;* the *Hebrews* were Shammai's future *Christians*. The author of *Acts* names his martyr "Stephen" to reveal Paul's heresy: "Stephen" is Greek for "crown."[46] NZR rendered *nezer* is also translated "crown."[47] NZR rendered *nazar* is translated "to separate."[48] NZR rendered *nazir* is translated "prince."[49]

> The *word of God* [Hebrew LHM] continued to spread; the number of the disciples increased greatly in Jerusalem, and a great many of the *priests became obedient to the faith* (Acts 6:7).

"The faith" is not Judaism or Paul's *Christianity* but the *Essene-Nazarene* reverence for "Father-Mother," the Elohim. Stephen is described as a man "full of grace and power" who "did great wonders and signs among the people" (Acts 6:8). *Acts* portrays Stephen in words also used to describe Jesus (John 1:14).

The story of Stephen shares elements with a significant event that occurred in Rome. Emperor Gaius (aka, *Caligula*) imprisoned Alexander "the Elabarak"[50] of Alexandria, reasons unknown, shortly before Gaius/"Caligula" was allegedly assassinated and Claudius elevated to Emperor, in January, 41 CE.[51] One of Claudius' first acts when he became Emperor was to release Philo's brother from prison.[52]

These parallel accounts connect "Stephen" and "Jesus" to "Alexander the Elabarak," a relationship that will become important in a moment.

Stephen, the "man who was crowned," is accused of speaking "blasphemous words against Moses and God," so he's arrested and taken before the council to be tried for heresy.

When the High Priest asks about the accusations against him, Stephen delivers the longest speech in the Bible, but it is riddled with mistakes that attract attention and raise questions. And the author of *Acts* wants Stephen to talk about *Abraham* and *El Shadday*:

> "Brothers and fathers, listen to me. The *God of glory* appeared to our ancestor *Abraham*... "(Acts 7:2).

At Gen 17:1-8, *El Shadday*, not YHWH, appeared to *Abram* and established a covenant with *Abraham*.

Shammai's version:

> "When Abram was ninety-nine years old, the LORD appeared **_TO_** Abram and said **_TO_** him, 'I am El Shadday...I will make my covenant between me and you and will greatly increase your numbers.'"

Hillel's version:

> "When Abram was ninety-nine years old YHWH did **_NOT_** appear. To Abram said, 'I am El Shadday...I will make my

covenant between me and you and will greatly increase your numbers.'"

The word which Shammai translates "to" is the Hebrew consonant L, but L can be correctly rendered in more than one way:

> L rendered *eL* is translated "to" and "God";[53]
> L rendered *Lo* is translated "not");[54]
> L rendered *aL* is also translated "not."[55]

The context determines the choice, and YHWH had **_not_** visited Abram since before Ishmael was born when Abram was eighty-six years old (Gen 16:16).

So, after at least thirteen years with no communication from YHWH, when Abram was nine-nine, he is approached by *El Shadday*, which the *House of Shammai* translates "God Almighty"[56] and the *House of Hillel* translates "God with breasts."[57] Stephen refers to Her as "God of Glory."[58]

The supporting "proof" that "God with breasts" is the correct translation is revealed in Jacob's blessing for his son Joseph, Gen 49:25-6:

> Because of **_your father's LHM,_** who helps you, [and] because of the **_Shadday_** who blesses you with blessings of...the **_breast and womb_**. Your father's blessings are greater than the blessings of the ancient mountains, than the bounty of the age-old hills. Let all these rest on the head of *Joseph, on the brow of the* **_nezir_** *among his brothers* (Gen 49:25-6; emphasis added).

Abraham's great-grandson Joseph is the first to be identified as NZR[59], establishing his superiority as "Prince" over all his brothers. Joseph's far-in-the-future "son" will be named "YaH-Zeus," not *Yehoshua* or *Yeshua*, but *YaH-Zeus*, the unification of Judean and Greco-Roman deities, and the title given to Essene High Priests.

The "God with breasts" says to Abram,

> "I will make my covenant between me and you, and will make you exceedingly numerous." Then Abram fell on his face; **eLaH eM** said, "As for me, this is my covenant with you: You shall be the ancestor of a multitude of nations. No longer shall your name be *Abram*, but your name shall be *Abraham*; for I have made you the ancestor of a multitude of nations...I will make nations of you, and **kings shall come from you**...And I will give to you, and to your offspring after you, the land where you are now an alien, all the land of Canaan for a perpetual holding; and **I will be their Elah Em, El, Elohim.**[60] (Gen 17:2-8; emphasis added).

This is the feature of Hillel's Judaism that has been hiding behind enigmas: *El* and *Elah* Mother, or *"God with breasts,"* are the Gods of *Abraham, Isaac,* and *Jacob*, and in a scene where he is about to die, "Stephen" exposes this Nazarene secret.

The name BRM, *aB RaM*, is translated "Father Exalted." His new name, *BRHM*, gives *Abraham* several new attributes:

Rendered *BaR Ha eM,* he is "Son of the Mother."
Rendered *aB RaHaM,* he is "Father of Compassion."
Rendered *aB ReHeM,* he is "Father of Womb."

Abram no longer exists to exalt King YHWH; as *Abraham* he now serves *Eloah and Elah Em*, "Father God and Goddess Mother."

Eventually, the deity with breasts addresses the problem of Sarai's barrenness:

> LHM said to Abraham, "As for Sarai your wife, you shall not call her *Sarai* but *Sarah* shall be her name. I will bless her, and moreover, I will give you a son by her. I will bless her, and she shall give rise to nations; *kings*

of peoples shall come from her" (Gen 17:15-16; emphasis added).

SRH is *iSha oRaH* and/or *aSha oRaH*, the reviled goddess *Asherah* whose name is perhaps a combination of *ish/isha* ("man/woman") and *oRaH* ("light"). The evidence reveals that aB'eL and iSha oRaH, NOT YaHWeH, possess the characteristics revered and adopted by Abraham, Isaac, Jacob, Joseph, and YaH-Zeus.

El Shadday appears to Jacob *after* Rachel has given birth to Joseph the NZR, but *before* she dies giving birth to Benjamin.

> "Your name is Jacob; no longer shall your name be called Jacob, but Israel[61] shall be your name." So his name was called Israel. And LHM said to him, "I am El Shadday: be fruitful and multiply; a nation and a company of nations shall come from you, and ***kings shall spring from you***" (Genesis 35:10-1; emphasis added).

Next, Stephen points to the Genesis 40 story, *The Triumph of Joseph at the Court of the Pharaoh:*

> Because the patriarchs were jealous of Joseph, they sold him as a slave into Egypt. But eLaH eM was with him and rescued him from all his troubles and granted Joseph favor and wisdom in the sight of Pharaoh king of Egypt, who appointed him *ruler over Egypt and all his household* (Acts 7:9-10).

Stephen doesn't reveal what eLaH eM did that motivated Pharaoh to reward Joseph so generously, but this story comes from Genesis, and it is about a baker who is sentenced to be crucified, the only crucifixion in the Hebrew Bible.

The critical climax to this crucifixion is carried in the string of Hebrew consonants at Genesis 40:22:

WTSRHPMTLHKSRPTRLHMYSP.

Shammai's rendering and translation:

We eT SaR Ha oPiM TaLaH KaSeR PaTaR LaHeM YowSeP,

translated,

"...but he hanged the chief baker, just as Joseph had interpreted to them."

Hillel's equally valid rendering and translation:

We eT iSha oRaH oPiM eT eLaH, KiSar PeTeR eLa Ha eM, YoSeP,

translated,

"...but the Woman of Light, 'Baker,' is Elah, Kisar's[62] firstling, Ela the Mother of Joseph."

Shammai's translation of Gen 40:23 is brief: "The chief cupbearer, however, did not remember Joseph; he forgot him."

Hillel's translation is incredibly important because it reveals that Joseph's Mother was *not* crucified (Genesis 40:23):

WLZKRSRHMMSQMTYWSPWYYSKHH

Hillel's rendering and translation:

We eL ZaKaR, iS RaHaM MeSeQ,[63] eM eT YoWSeP, WaY YiSKa HeHu,

translated, "

"But God is male, *a man with womb acquired* Mother of Joseph, but [she is] forgotten."

Apparently, Joseph's "God-Mother," also known as "the Baker," professed that "she" was a "he," but with a *womb* instead of a *penis*. A strange story, indeed, but a parallel is found in first-century Rome where the *Ides of March* was the annual celebration of the death and resurrection of the god, *Attis*.

According to one version of the myth, Attis grew into a godlike, long-haired beauty, whereupon Cybele his mother fell in love with him. So Attis' foster parents sent him far away to Pessinus, where he was to wed the king's daughter.

Just as the marriage-song was being sung, Cybele appeared in her transcendent power, and Attis went mad and castrated himself under a pine tree.

In 1867, a life-size statue of Attis was discovered at the *Campus of the Magna Mater*, at Ostia Antica. It was constructed between 275 and 300 CE, before Nicene Christianity became the official religion of the Roman Empire and all others became heresies deserving of death.

"The actual shrine was added in the third quarter of the third century at the south-east side...The reliefs have been dated to the second half of the third century...damaged on purpose, presumably by Christians...In the apse is a plaster cast of a statue of a reclining Attis, after the emasculation. In his left hand is a shepherd's crook, in his right hand a pomegranate. His head is crowned with bronze rays of the sun and on his Phrygian cap is a crescent moon...Attis was regarded as a solar deity and identified with the moon-god Men. He is leaning on a bust, probably the personification of the river Gallos, where he had died...The statue is a dedication by Caius Cartilius Euplus, witness the inscription on the plinth: "To the divine majesty of Attis, Caius Cartilius Euplus, after an admonition by the goddess."[64]

Chapter Seven

The Watchtower

After Attis castrates himself, he is a god without a penis, a notable parallel to Joseph's *Baker-Mother* in Genesis. Also notable, Julius Caesar was assassinated on the first day of the *Ides of March*, 44 BCE; Emperor Tiberius Julius Caesar died on the second day of the *Ides of March*, 37 CE. Both were considered "gods," which suggests that, perhaps, like Attis, they were "resurrected" into new lives.

It appears that the *Ides of March* was a very important celebration in Julio-Claudian Rome. It also appears that a "god without a penis" was a popular motif. Perhaps these unique "gods" were created to disguise women in positions of power among societies that demeaned women and rejected a goddess—to the point of killing them.

"He's a God, He just doesn't have a penis!"

According to *The Gospel of Thomas*, "Jesus" had an understanding of this tradition:

> "Simon Peter said... 'Let's put Mary out of our group, for women are not worthy of life.' Jesus replied, '...*I myself will lead her to make her male, so that even she may become a live spirit...*'"[65]

The Gospel According to Mark is generally accepted as the first of the three synoptics to be written. While working on the Dead Sea Scrolls in 1963, Jean Carmignac translated Mark from Greek to Hebrew and was surprised to discover that the project pointed to Greek Mark as a translation from a Hebrew or Aramaic original.[66]

Carmignac proposed that the earliest version of Mark was composed in Biblical Hebrew, a theory most scholars reject. (Evidence to follow supports Carmignac.)

A date for Mark has been elusive because the Early Church Fathers appear determined to minimize its importance—and may have planned to destroy it altogether.

Mark could have been written as early as 37 BCE, after Herod became King of Judea with the Hasmonean princess Mariame as his Queen. The festivals in Alexandria that celebrated *Isis and Osiris* and the *Hilaria* in Rome that celebrated *Cybele and Attis* were well known throughout the Roman Empire. Both offered annual celebrations to honor the god and goddess.

The *House of Shammai* celebrated *Passover* and looked forward to the fulfillment of the *Bethlehem Prophecy* (Micah 5:2-3):

> But you, **Bethlehem Ephrathah**,
> though you are small among the clans of Judah,
> out of you will come for me
> one who will be ruler over Israel,
> whose origins are from of old,
> from ancient times.
> ³ Therefore Israel will be abandoned
> until the time when she who is in labor bears a son,
> and the rest of his brothers return
> to join the Israelites.

The *House of Hillel* could claim an equivalent Old Testament event and a related prophecy. The event was the crucifixion of the Goddess-Baker who metamorphosed into a God without a penis; the prophecy is Micah 4:8-10, the *Watchtower Prophecy* (Hillel's Version):

> And you, O ***Watchtower of the flock,***
> O stronghold of the Daughter of Zion,
> the former dominion will be restored to you;
> sovereignty will come to the ***Daughter of Jerusalem.***"
> Why do you now cry aloud?
> Is there no king among you?
> Has your counselor perished so that anguish grips you
> like a woman in labor?
> Writhe in agony, Daughter Zion, like a woman in labor,
> for now you must leave the city to camp in the open field.
> ***You will go to Babylon;***
> ***there you will be rescued from YHWH***
> ***and the hand of your enemies.***

In Hebrew, "watchtower" is *MGDL*, rendered *MiGDoL* and/or *MaGDaL*, the obvious inspiration for Jesus' companion, "The Magdalene."

The *Bethlehem Prophecy* is still celebrated in YHWH's Christian churches but the *Watchtower Prophecy* is virtually unknown—by design, of course.

Two glaring omissions in Mark that are prominent in Matthew and Luke are the birth of Jesus in *Bethlehem* to the *Virgin Mother*. Scholars' solution to these omissions is to invent a Q Gospel that Matthew and Luke could have plagiarize while also plagiarizing Mark.

However, Carmignac's proposal offers a simpler, more logical solution. Matthew 2:23 claims that "Jesus" was called "the Nazarene" because he came from "Nazareth." Mark 1:9 says, "Jesus came from *Nazareth*..." supporting Mt 2:23.

However, a *Hebrew* Mark that says, "Jesus came from *BTLHM*" restores both the town *BeTLeHeM* and the *Virgin Mother* (*BeTuLaH eM*), evidence that supports Carmignac's proposal and exposes Matthew as a Christian interpolator—

and the reason Polycarp may have been willing to risk execution to unmask him.

BTLHM also reveals *The Virgins'* ultimate secret: they were believed to be **BaT** *eLaH eM*, "Daughters of God the Mother," descendants of *SaRaH*, also known as "aSaRaH," the Nazarene version of the Sumerian goddess, "KiSaR." This is the bloodline that El Shadday proclaimed would produce "Kings and Queens."

Julius *Caesar* is identified as a descendant of *Kisar*.[67] The Caesars believed Kisar came to Earth from Venus, thus the monuments honoring Venus and her depictions on their coins.

What else in *Ur-Marcus* was excised or changed? Most notably, all the events that follow the crucifixion. The earliest surviving texts end with Jesus' body being taken to the tomb never to be seen again.

But only after a revealing crucifixion scene:

> ...Jesus cried out with a loud voice, "Eloi, Eloi... (Mark 15:34).

Eloi is the Aramaic word for "my God." Mark's Nazarene original was more likely, *Elah, Elah*, "Goddess, Goddess!"

Chapter Eight

From Julius Caesar to Hillel

Nicholas of Damascus and Plutarch sprinkled enigmatic clues into their versions of Julius Caesar's assassination that identify Cleopatra as a participant:

> *Tyche* had a part in this by causing Caesar himself to set a certain day on which the members of the Senate were to assemble to consider certain motions which he wished to introduce. When the appointed day came the conspirators assembled, prepared in all respects.[68]

A coin minted in the first century BCE—*in Damascus*—associates *Tyche* with Cleopatra:

> The...ancient bronze was struck in Damascus, Syria ...probably between 33-32 BC... Of particular interest is the obverse depiction of Tyche, *whose features unmistakably resemble Cleopatra...The motif of Cleopatra as Tyche probably intended to advertise the queen's responsibility for the prosperity of her subjects*. (Image copied from coins for sale by Etsy[69]).

It seems more likely that the coin was struck in Damascus to help decipher Nicholaus' enigmatic tale of Julius Caesar's "assassination."

Nicolaus was also in Alexandria with Antony and Cleopatra but relocated to Jerusalem to serve Herod and Mariame after the suicides.[70]

> ..[Julius Caesar's] friends were alarmed at certain rumors and tried to stop him going to the Senate-house, as did his doctors, for he was suffering from one of his occasional dizzy spells. His wife, Calpurnia, especially, who was frightened by some visions in her dreams, clung to him and said that she would not let him go out that day. But Brutus, one of the conspirators who was then thought of as a firm friend, came up and said, "What is this, Caesar? Are you a man to pay attention to a woman's dreams and the idle gossip of stupid men, and to insult the Senate by not going out, although it has honored you and has been specially summoned by you? But listen to me, cast aside the forebodings of all these people, and come. The Senate has been in session waiting for you since early this morning." This swayed Caesar and he left.
>
> Before he entered the chamber, the priests brought up the victims for him to make what was to be his last sacrifice. The omens were clearly unfavorable. After this unsuccessful sacrifice, the priests made repeated other ones, to see if anything more propitious might appear than what had already been revealed to them. In the end they said that they could not clearly see the divine intent, for there was some transparent, malignant spirit hidden in the victims. Caesar was annoyed and abandoned divination till sunset, though the priests continued all the more with their efforts.
>
> Those of the murderers present were delighted at all this, though Caesar's friends asked him to put off the

meeting of the Senate for that day because of what the priests had said, and he agreed to do this. But some attendants came up, calling him and saying that the Senate was full. He glanced at his friends, but Brutus approached him again and said, "Come, good sir, pay no attention to the babblings of these men, and *do not postpone what Caesar and his Dynamis[71] has seen fit to arrange.* Make your own courage your favorable omen."

It is this revelation in the earliest source of Caesar's assassination to which Luc Plutarchus would later lend support when he identifies "Dynamis" as the one who "was guiding the action."[72] Notably, it was another "Luc," the gospel writer, who identifies "Dynamis" as the "messenger" who informs the Virgin Mary that she would give birth to the "son of Theos" (Luke 1:35).

Nicolas of Damascus continues:

> He convinced Caesar with these words, took him by the right hand, and led him to the Senate which was quite near. Caesar followed in silence.
>
> The Senate rose in respect for his position when they saw him entering. *Those who were to have part in the plot stood near him*. Right next to him went Tillius Cimber, whose brother had been exiled by Caesar. Under pretext of a humble request on behalf of this brother, Cimber approached and grasped the mantle of his toga, seeming to want to make a more positive move with his hands upon Caesar. Caesar wanted to get up and use his hands, but was prevented by Cimber and became exceedingly annoyed.
>
> That was the moment for the men to set to work. All quickly unsheathed their daggers and rushed at him **["him" who? Caesar or Cimber?]** First Servilius Casca struck him with the point of the blade on the left shoulder a little above the collar-bone. He had been aiming for that, but in the excitement he missed.

[Wait! Did he strike him or did he miss?] Caesar rose to defend himself, and in the uproar Casca shouted out in Greek to his brother. The latter heard him and drove his sword into the ribs [whose ribs?]. After a moment, Cassius made a slash at his face, and Decimus Brutus pierced him in the side [pierced who? Cimber? Brutus? Caesar?]. While Cassius Longinus was trying to give him another blow he missed and struck Marcus Brutus on the hand. Minucius also hit out at Caesar and hit Rubrius in the thigh. They were just like men doing battle against him.[73]

Then, after these meticulously detailed swings and misses, with the attackers suffering more injuries than Caesar, Nicolaus drops the clue that opens the door through which Julius Casar leaves Rome and enters the realm of Nazarene Judaism in Jerusalem.

> Under the mass of wounds, he fell at the foot of Pompey's statue. Everyone wanted *to seem* to have had some part in the murder, and there was not one of them who failed to strike his body as it lay there, until, **wounded thirty-five times**, he breathed his last.[74]

Caesar, surrounded by his closest friends and staunchest supporters—but blocked from view by the others—certainly should have been dead. As with any good performance, plenty of blood was probably spilled—but none of it was Caesar's. In fact, it's unlikely that it was human blood.

As with all "gods," Caesar was a candidate for metamorphosis. And "thirty-five," which is **thirty-six minus one**, is a message meant for *Gnostic-Nazarene Initiates* that tells them where he went:

The Hebrew words *Zadokim Nistarim* ("hidden righteous ones") and/or *Lamed Vav Zadokim* ("36 righteous ones")[75] refers to 36 Righteous people, a notion rooted within mystical Judaism, the secret version that was practiced by the Nazarenes. The singular form is *Zadok Nistar*), and/or *Zadok An Ishtar*, translated "Righteous An Ishtar." In Mesopotamian myth, Ansar is Ishtar's father, the earliest members of the family Julius Caesar claimed as ancestors.

> It is said that *at all times there are 36 special people in the world*, and that were it not for them, all of them, *if even one of them was missing*, the world would come to an end. The two Hebrew letters for 36 are the lamed, which is 30, and the vav, which is 6. Therefore, these 36 are referred to as the Lamed-Vav Zaddikim.[76] This widely held belief, this most unusual Jewish concept, is based on a Talmudic statement to the effect that in every generation 36 righteous people 'greet the Shechinah,'[77] the Divine Presence (Tractate Sanhedrin 97b; Tractate Sukkah 45b).
>
> The *Lamed-Vav Zaddikim* are also called the Nistarim[78] ("concealed ones"). They emerge from their self-imposed concealment and, by the mystic powers which they possess, *they succeed in averting the threatened disasters of a people persecuted by the enemies that surround them*. They return to their anonymity as soon as their task is accomplished, 'concealing' themselves once again in a Jewish community wherein they are relatively unknown.[79]

The number 36 is twice 18. In Jewish numerology ("gematria"), the number 18 stands for "life," because the Hebrew letters that spell chai, meaning "living," add up to 18. Because 36 = 2×18, it represents "two lives."[80]

The "two lives" in the story of the assassination are *Gaius Julius Caesar* and *Hillel the Elder*, among the most significant of any two lives in history. The "threatened disaster" was the rejection of the Nazarenes' "Daughter Jerusalem" by the Patriarchal Judean Priests. Annual festivals would have been performed in Jerusalem, just as they were in Alexandria and Rome, to tell the story of "YH-Zeus son of Joseph the NZR."

Plutarch's version of Julius Caesar's assassination solidifies the identity of the genius behind Caesar's metamorphosis into Hillel:

> Caesar took the roll and would have read it, but was prevented by the multitude of people who engaged his attention, although he set out to do so many times, and holding in his hand and retaining that roll alone, he passed on into the senate.
>
> These things may have happened of their own accord; the place, however, which was the scene of that struggle and murder, and in which the senate was then assembled, since it contained a statue of Pompey and had been dedicated by Pompey as an additional ornament to his ***theatre***, made it wholly clear that it was the work of some ***Ouranios Dynamis*** which was calling and guiding the action.[81]

Tucked within the last sentence is the enigma that carries the literal history. The "theatrics" that were played out were "the work of Ouranios **Dynamis** that was guiding the action." And that "heavenly power" was wielded by the goddess in this narrative, identified as "Dynamis," wife of King Asander and mother of *Tiberius Julius Aspurgus Philoromaios*,[82] the family better known as Julius Caesar, Cleopatra, and their son *Caesarion*, aka, *Emperor Tiberius*.

What is Plutarch's message–the foremost fact in this fable?

Julius and Cleopatra were behind the faked assassination of the *Divine Julius son of Venus* on the *Ides of March*.

Why would they want to fake his death?

One reason for faking someone's death is because a dead person can't be assassinated. Furthermore, the wars for control of Rome–whether factual or fictional–had been won; the duties of Rome's leader could be safely passed on to Julius' descendants. All that remained unresolved was the war that was still being waged between Orthodox and Hellenized Jews.

Julius Caesar died—really died—c. 17 BCE. At the time of his death he was called *Asander Philocaesar Philoromaios* ("lover of Kisar Lover of Rome"). *Asander* is a derivative of *Alexander*, a reference to his ancestor, Alexander the Great.

Evidence suggests this coin was minted by *Augustus*, also known as *Octavian* (Latin for "eight"), c. 17 BCE, concurrent with the death of *Asander*, also known as *Julius Caesar* and *Hillel the Elder*.

The eight-pointed star is the ancient symbol for Venus. The flames may represent the bloodline of the Ish and Ishshah who came to Earth from Venus, the "Perpetual Fire" preserved by the Israelite Temple Virgins.[83]

Nicolaus credits Caesar's assassination to *Tyche* and mints a coin with the image of Cleopatra as Tyche. Plutarch credits Caesar's assassination to *Dynamis*; *Dynamis Philoromaios*, King Asander's wife, Queen of the Bosporus Empire.

Archaeologists have found three statues that Dynamis dedicated to herself; another was erected in honor of Livia Drusilla. In Phanagoria (a peninsula in the area of the Black Sea and the Sea of Azov), Dynamis dedicated an inscription honoring Augustus as, "The emperor, Caesar, son of Theos, the Theos Augustus, the overseer of every land and sea."

In another inscription at the same location Dynamis refers to herself as "Empress and friend to Rome." In the temple of Aphrodite, Dynamis dedicated a statue of Livia, and the inscription refers to Livia as the "Empress and benefactress of Dynamis."[84]

An early first century CE bust of Empress Livia was discovered at Arsinoe, Egypt, and Cleopatra's younger sister was "Arsinoe." Dynamis seems to have gone to great lengths to identify *Empress Livia* as Cleopatra's younger sister Arsinoe. And in doing so she also ties a thread from herself to Cleopatra; she died c. 8 CE.

Julius Caesar initiated the *Ludi Victoriae Caesaris* in 46 BCE to dedicate his Temple of Venus and to affirm that he was descended from Venus through Iulus, the son of Aeneas. Vergil wrote the *Aeneid* to emphasize this connection between the Julii bloodline and Venus–the planet and the goddess. The name, *Vergil*, can be associated with "Virgins of El."

When King Asander died in 17 BCE, Augustus reinstated the *Secular Games* and money maker *M. Sanquinius* fashioned coins that depict a comet over the head of a wreathed man, assumed to be Julius Caesar. Concurrent with Asander's death, a pyramid was built in Rome large enough for two.[85]

Suetonius reports that shortly after Julius was assassinated in 44 BCE, and just as the *Ludi Victoriae Caesaris* was getting underway, "a comet shone for seven successive days, rising about the eleventh hour, and was believed to be the soul of Caesar."[86]

Conclusion:

"YH-Zeus" is the name given to the resurrected "Son of Joseph the Nazar," an attempt to unify the Judean's *YHWH* with *Zeus* and restore reverence for the Great Mother, the *Feminine Energy contribution to Creation*.

Support for our hypothesis that Antony and Cleopatra metamorphosed into Herod and Mariame after the Battle of Actium may be found tucked away on page 82, footnote 39, in Duane Roller's *The World of Juba II and Kleopatra Selene*:

> The [children's] tutors Euphronios and Rhodon disappear from the record at this time... (Plutarch, Antonius 81). Conspicuously absent in these last days is *Nikolaos of Damaskos*, who may have been successful in suppressing his role, or more likely, had wisely fled to *Herod in Judea, beginning forty years of service to that dynasty, and thus saving both his life and his career.* In fact, a number of scholars and intellectuals moved from the Alexandrian court to Judea at this time.[87]

The children's tutors along with the "scholars and intellectuals" moved from Cleopatra's palace in Alexandria to Herod's palace in Judea where the dramas continued to unfold and enigmas continued to pour forth.

Plutarch warned that "stories about gods"[88] could not be read literally, and he left a blatant clue about the suicide myth at the conclusion of *Life of Antony*:

> But others say that the asp was kept carefully shut up in a water jar, and that while Cleopatra was stirring it up and irritating it with a golden distaff it sprang and fastened itself upon her arm. **But the truth of the matter no one knows;** for it was also said that she carried about poison in a hollow comb and kept the comb hidden in her hair; and yet neither spot nor other sign of poison broke out upon her body.[89]

Chapter Nine

The Relic of Christ

Decades before the author of *Acts* invented "Stephen" to leave clues that might preserve the story of *YH-Zeus the Nazarene* and his relationship to a crucified Baker in Genesis, a member of the Julio-Claudian dynasty commissioned a cameo that was part of a shipment—described as "Relics of Christ"—that included the *Crown of Thorns* and the *Image of Edessa*.

The cameo was shipped to Paris from the treasury of the Byzantine Empire. Baldwin II, emperor of the Latin Empire of Constantinople, sold it to Louis IX of France, where it is listed in the 1279 inventory of Sainte-Chapelle in Paris.[90]

Philip VI of France sent it to Pope Clement VI in Avignon in 1342 or 1343 possibly as collateral for financial support. In 1363, Antipope Clement VII then returned it to Charles V of France. The cameo was then brought to Saint-Chapelle in 1379.[91]

In 1620, the antiquary *Nicolas-Claude Fabri de Peiresc* recognized that the cameo depicted Julio-Claudians; it was quickly renamed, "Great Cameo of France." In 1792, Louis XVI of France claimed the cameo and took it to the *Cabinet des médailles* in order to protect it from the French revolutionaries.[92]

The cameo is listed on the 1279 invoice as,

"Triumph of Joseph at the Court of the Pharaoh."

A multitude of opinions regarding the identities of the characters have been proposed and debated since its discovery, but no consensus has been reached.

The proposed choices have been complicated by the assumption that a Julio-Claudian "death" meant an actual death, which was not always the case. Sometimes a "metamorphosis," common in gods of mythology,[93] gave them another identity and different tasks to complete, a new challenge for Philo-curious historians to tackle.

All the members of the Julio-Claudian Dynasty were portrayed as gods and goddesses; therefore, as Plutarch attempted to explain, stories written about them cannot be read literally, a suggestion historians reject without discussion and often with ridicule.

The items depicted with the characters identify them.

In the heavens, the deceased (left to right):

Marcus Antonius holds the shield of a Roman general; *Augustus* holds the staff of the emperor; *Cleopatra* holds the *Eye of Ra; Julius Caesar* rides Pegasus, a reference to his beloved horse which only he could ride.[94]

The small figure between Augustus and Julius Caesar is the *Lares of Augustus*, "identified with the inaugural day of Imperial Roman magistracies and with Augustus himself."[95]

The "inaugural day" this Cameo celebrates is Claudius' elevation to Emperor after the removal of Gaius Caesar Augustus Germanicus, who was assassinated (allegedly) on January 24, 41 CE. Gaius was nicknamed, "Caligula."

Middle row (left to right):
Julia the Younger holding her nephew, the future emperor Nero; the couple staring lovingly at one another is Germanicus and wife, Agrippina I; Emperor Tiberius holds the staff of the emperor; Empress Livia sits on her throne; Claudius is shown reaching for the emperor's staff with his wife Agrippina II standing at his side.

The questions to be answered are, why is this cameo part of a shipment identified as "Relics of Christ"?

And why is it listed on the invoice as "Triumph of Joseph and the Court of the Pharaoh"?

In 41 CE Rome, Claudius was chosen to be emperor, but Tiberius is shown handing the *Shield of Zeus and Pallas Athena* to Germanicus and Agrippina, and he is *not* handing the Emperor's Staff to Claudius.

Why?

Germanicus and Agrippina *metamorphosed* into the *defacto* rulers identified by historians as the freedmen, *Tiberius Claudius Narcissus*[96] *and Marcus Antonius Pallas.*[97]

During Jerusalem's annual celebrations of the *Triumph of Joseph at the Court of the Pharoah*, they played the roles of

YaH-Zeus the Nazarene and Mary the Magdala.

In Alexandria, this couple was known as siblings, *Alexander the Elah BaRaK*, (translated, "Goddess Blessed") and Philo (translated, "love"), [98] a "Pythagorean Jew," also known as "Mary the Watchtower."

> "Jesus replied, '...*I myself will lead her to make her male*, so that even she may become a live spirit...'"[99]

In Jerusalem as *President of the Great Sanhedrin* and while teaching in the *House of Hillel*, "Germanicus" was called *Gamaliel*, Hebrew GMLL, rendered *GaMa eL eLa* and translated, "Within (is) God and Goddess."

The Nazarenes at Mount Carmel never ceased praising "Father-Mother." They rejected YHWH and continued to honor the *Nazarene Holy Trinity*, the *Elohim*, introduced at Gen 1:1.

Hillel brought *Father-Mother* out from hiding when he established his school in Jerusalem alongside Shammai's.

The people were given a choice, and some preferred the simplicity of an authoritarian's "dos and don'ts"—with vicarious atonement—over the challenge of making wise decisions monitored by benevolent parents who taught,

> "For every action there is an equal and opposite reaction; therefore, treat others the way you want to be treated."

"Matthew," aka, Paulus rejected *Jesus the Nazarene* and invented *Jesus from Nazareth*. The *Israelites* who survived the purging at Mount Carmel went into hiding and were renamed *Issenes*, Philo's "Essenes, whose High Priests and Priestesses are identified as "those who are crowned," *Nazarenes*.

Polycarp titled *The Gospel According to Marcus* to identify *Marcus* (*Antonius* or *Agrippa*) as its author, prior to his death c. 12 BCE.

The Gospel According to Matthew identifies the false apostle *Paulus* as its author. In Greek, "mathétés" is translated "disciple," and according to *Acts*, Paul was Gamaliel's "disciple":

> I, indeed, am a man, a Jew...and brought up in this city *at the feet of Gamaliel*, having been taught according to the exactness of a *law of the fathers*..." (Acts 2:23).

Polycarp also left clues to the historical identity of Paulus, and he reveals a physical feature of the Nazarene's sons:

> Now in the church at Antioch there were *prophets and teachers*: Barnabas, Simeon called **Niger**, Lucius of **Cyrene**, Manaen (who had been brought up with Herod the tetrarch), and **Saul**. While they were *performing a public duty for the Emperor*[100] and fasting, the **Holy Spirit** said, "Set apart for me *Barnabas and Saul* for the work to which I have called them." And after they had fasted and prayed, they laid their hands on them and sent them off. So Barnabas and **Saul**, sent

forth by the *Holy Spirit*, went down to Seleucia and sailed from there to Cyprus. When they arrived at Salamis, they proclaimed the word of *God* in the Jewish synagogues. And John was with them as their helper (Acts 13:1-5).

The name listed first is *Barnabas* identifying him, enigmatically, as the "son of" (*Bar*) an important "father" (*abas*). No "father" would have been more important than "Jesus," and a "Bar Jesus" is featured in the next section of *Acts*.

Simeon called Niger is identified as having dark skin (*niger* is translated "black"[101]); Antony and Cleopatra's daughter Selene married Juba II, a North African, with whom she had children whose skin would have been "niger." Hillel's son was *Simeon ben Hillel* and his great-grandson (Gamaliel's son), was *Simeon ben Gamaliel,* or "Simeon called Niger."

Lucius of Cyrene reveals that he, too, is from North Africa, and Paul refers to him as a "kinsman" (Romans 16:21).

Apparently, the author of Acts thought it was important to convey the information that people of color were among Hillel's influential descendants.

Antioch was the third largest city of the Roman Empire in size and importance (after Rome and Alexandria). It is the logical choice to begin the project of convincing Judeans and Israelites—whose ancestors had been deceived into worshipping YHWH—to return to Elohim, "Father-Mother." And their kinsman, Saul, was with them—until he wasn't.

> They traveled through the whole island as far as Paphos, where they found a *Jewish sorcerer and false prophet named **Bar-Jesus**,* an attendant of the proconsul, ***Sergius Paulus***. The proconsul, a man of intelligence, summoned Barnabas and ***Saul*** because he wanted to hear *the word of **LHM***. But Elymas the sorcerer (for that is what his name means) opposed them and tried to turn the proconsul from the faith.

> *Then Saul, who was also called Paulus*, filled with the Holy Spirit, looked directly at Elymas and said, "*O child of the devil* and enemy of all righteousness, you are full of all kinds of deceit and trickery! Will you never stop perverting the straight ways of YHWH? Now look, the hand of YHWH is against you, and for a time you will be blind and unable to see the light of the sun." Immediately *mist and darkness came over him*, and he groped about, **seeking someone to lead him by the hand**. When the proconsul saw what had happened, he believed, for he was *astonished at the teaching about YHWH* (Acts 13:6-12).

According to *Act's* first version of Saul's vision of Jesus, it is Paul who is blinded and led by the hand. This dispute at Paphos that culminates in someone's blindness is between *Bar-Jesus* and *Saulus*, the man who participated in the stoning of Stephen.

The author of *Acts* recounts three *contradictory* versions of Saul's vision of Jesus on the road to Damascus.[102] In the first (Acts 9:1-19), he uses the same word, *cheiragōgous* – translated, "led him by the hand" – when describing Saul's encounter with Bar-Jesus.

The sentence structure and choice of pronouns leaves it unclear which man is blinded after Saul hurls damning words at *Bar-Jesus* and his "devil-father" *Jesus*.

But the author of *Acts* has already identified the man who is blinded and "led by the hand" at the time of his claimed conversion. It is Saulus, the man who attempts to damn Bar-Jesus to blindness and who was placed at the stoning of Stephen.

Paul seems unaware of any of *Acts'* three contradictory versions of his conversion when he describes the experience in his second letter to the Corinthians.[103] The dramatic blindness scene, being led by the hand, and Ananias' miraculous healing and significant baptism are not mentioned–qualifying as "noteworthy omissions" (Philo's Rule 19).

According to Shammai's Jews, *The Way* was a heresy and *YaH-Zeus* was a "false prophet." Perhaps the "son of YaH-Zeus," had been sent to Paphos to guard Lucius Sergius Paulus and to try to convince him to reject *YHWH* and embrace *El and Elah*.

When Claudius became Emperor in 41, Narcissus arranged for Vespasian to be appointed *Legate of Legio II Augusta,* in Germania.[104] And at about the same time, an inscription identifies *Lucius Sergius Paulus* and others as being in charge of maintaining the banks and channels of the Tiber River. It reads in part:

"...L. Sergius Paullus...curators of the river Tiberis... Claudius Caesar.[105] (Claudius was Emperor of Rome from 41 until 54.)

The name "Sergius" comes from the Latin word *servare,* defined as, "to make safe...*keep unharmed...guard... protect...rescue.*"[106] Perhaps this "Lucius Paulus" had been sent to Paphos to protect him from punishment for an act against one of the Julio-Claudians, i.e., a *Nazar* whom Polycarp calls "crowned."

Julia the Younger (left holding Nero) married Lucius Aemilus Paulus, her first half-cousin, a marriage arranged by Emperor Augustus c. 5 or 6 BCE. They had a daughter and a son, but the son is something of a mystery:

> Paullus and Julia had a daughter, Aemilia Lepida, and possibly a son, Marcus Aemilius Lepidus (although he may instead have been the son to Marcus Aemilius Lepidus).[107]

Julia was exiled to a small Italian island c. 8 CE for an adulterous affair that produced a child. Augustus ordered her to leave the baby on a mountainside to die, an order she did not obey.[108]

Julia's husband *Lucius Paulus* was convicted of a conspiracy in a revolt and was executed (or exiled?) between 1 and 14 CE.[109]

Julia and Paulus' "possible" son was "possibly" called "Marcus Aemilius Lepidus." Where's the "Paulus" in his name?

> Some areas of his lineage are unclear. He was possibly the son of consul **Lucius Aemilius Paullus**. If so, he was also great-grandson of Lucius Aemilius Lepidus Paullus (consul of 50 BC and brother of the triumvir Marcus Aemilius Lepidus), and through his mother Julia the Younger, Lepidus was the great grandson of Emperor Augustus. It is also possible that he was instead the son of **Marcus Aemilius Lepidus the consul of 6 AD**.[110]

Another prominent Julio-Claudian's biography is notably incomplete. *Gaius Caesar Augustus Germanicus*, better known as "Caligula," was Roman emperor from 37 until his alleged assassination in 41. He was [reportedly] "the son of the Roman general Germanicus and Augustus' granddaughter Agrippina the Elder, members of the first ruling family of the Roman Empire."[111]

Historians emphasize:

Of the few surviving sources about Caligula and his four-year reign, most were written by members of the nobility and senate, long after the events they purport to describe. For the early part of his reign, he is said to have been "good, generous, fair and community-spirited" but increasingly self-indulgent, cruel, sadistic, extravagant and sexually perverted thereafter; an insane, murderous tyrant who demanded and received worship as a living god, humiliated his Senate, and planned to make his horse a consul. Most modern commentaries seek to explain Caligula's position, personality and historical context. Some historians dismiss many of the allegations against him as misunderstandings, exaggeration, mockery or malicious fantasy.[112]

Suetonius quotes from a letter, which he attributes to Augustus Caesar, written to Agrippina the Elder. It reads:

> Yesterday I arranged with Talarius and Asillius to bring your boy Gaius on the fifteenth day before the Kalends of June, if it be *the will of the gods*. I send with him besides one of my slaves who is a physician, and I have written Germanicus to *keep him* if he wishes. Farewell, my own Agrippina, and take care to come in good health to your Germanicus.[113]

Augustus informs granddaughter Agrippina that he had written to her husband Germanicus (also known as *Gamaliel*) to tell him he could "keep him" if he wished. Were it not for the *striking statement* "will of the gods" (Philo's Rule 20), it might be assumed that "him" refers to "the slave who is a physician." However, because a signal for enigma *is* inserted, it is more likely that "him" refers to Gaius.

This suggests that Germanicus and Agrippina are not Gaius' biological parents and that he came to them via

Agrippina's grandfather Augustus. It also hints that Gaius may have been under the care of a physician.

Suetonius also provides two name clues: "Talarius" and "Asillius." Talaria are the winged boots worn by the Greek god Hermes. And a Hermes thread is conspicuous in *Acts*: "Barnabas they called Zeus, and *Paul they called Hermes*, because he was the chief speaker" (Acts 14:12).[114] Matching boot threads lead back to Gaius; the nickname "Caligula" is derived from the Latin word *caligae*, which also means "boots."

However, Talarius is not alone in arranging the adoption of Gaius. Suetonius identifies a second person, "Asillius," a name that is just one letter shy of the word *basillius*.

Basilius (Basileus) and the feminine Basilissa, resurrected for Alexander the Great and the Ptolemies of Egypt including Cleopatra, came to designate the Roman Emperor in the everyday and literary speech of the Greek-speaking Eastern Mediterranean during the time of Tiberius.[115]

And so it seems that Suetonius composed Augustus Caesar's letter to identify the people who arranged for the adoption of Gaius.[116] The first person named, "Talarius" can be tied to Hermes, and Polycarp associates Hermes with Paul (Acts 14:12). Therefore, it appears that Talarius is related in some way to Paul. But what is the relationship?

The Church was highly motivated to hide the relationship between Paul and the Julio-Claudians, and the works of Suetonius and Tacitus that would be helpful to historians were heavily edited. The fact that Lucius Paulus' son could be "either" *Lucius* or *Marcus* attests to the confusion wrought by editors with agendas. The "Marcus" possibility is because Lucius Paulus' brother was Marcus Paulus, and Lucius' son could have been Marcus' son. Either would have been a "Paulus."

It bears repeating: Agrippina's younger sister, Julia Vipsania *Paulus*, had a son who was left a virtual orphan when she was exiled c. 8 CE. His "possible" father, Marcus Aemilius Paulus was consul in 6 CE. Julia's son disappears from history when she is exiled with nothing more written about his fate.

The letter from Augustus to Agrippina seems to suggest that she and Germanicus (aka *Gamaliel*) agreed to take "Gaius" into their home.

> Paul says, 'I, indeed, am a man, a Jew...and brought up in this city *at the feet of Gamaliel,* [aka Germanicus] having been taught according to the exactness of a *law of the fathers*...' (Acts 2:23).

Julia the Younger's husband *Lucius Aemilius Paulus* was convicted of a plot to assassinate Augustus and was allegedly executed.[117] Notably, the *Lucius Paulus* at Paphos is given a middle name that identifies him as a man who was "guarded" and "kept unharmed."

Paulus at Paphos is Polycarp's enigmatic message that the man who was raised at the feet of *Gamaliel*, identified as "God and Goddess within," turned against the father of Bar Jesus, reunited with his own father, and set about to replace "Father-Mother" with YHWH and the ever-popular *vicarious atonement*.

Chapter Ten

The Middle Finger

The absence of Julia's husband on the Cameo is to be expected because of his plot to assassinate Augustus. He may have been suspected of counseling his son "Saul," aka, "Paul," to imprison and execute "Stephen," aka, "Alexander the Elabarak," aka, "Germanicus," aka, "Gamaliel," aka, "Jesus the Nazarene."

Lucius and Julia's son, Marcus or Lucius Paulus, sits in the foreground, barely visible but obviously dejected. Empress

Livia reveals with a gesture her opinion of him. And yes, the middle finger was a thing in the Roman Empire.[118]

The Nazarene's project to peacefully convert superstitious and fear-driven Israelites to the peaceful, loving arms of "Father-Mother" went well until Gamaliel's disciple "Paulus" chose to support his biological father, *Lucius Aemilius Paulus*, a disgraced Julio-Claudian and a promoter of the authoritarian, misogynistic *YHWH*.

Paulus, also known as *Matthew*, was Jerusalem's High Priest in 65-6.[119] He had unfettered access to Mark's script, performed during the annual celebration of *Joseph's Triumph*. He invented "Jesus from Nazareth," composed a nativity story, demonized King Herod, and added a post-crucifixion resurrection.

He then reworked Mark's text to support his invention, changing BTLHM to Nazareth and excising the celebration of the return of the Goddess-Mother and the Watchtower.

To preserve the popular vicarious atonement, the *blood of the Lamb* was replaced by the *blood of YH-Zeus*, a fiction that was successfully sold as fact to trusting souls who already believed YHWH was the only God, thanks to Elijah.

Fortunately for those who want to find *The Historical Jesus*—and the messages he tried to deliver—the Victor's version serves as Polycarp's *Trojan Horse*.

CHAPTER ELEVEN

Juba's Daughter

Two inscriptions excavated in Athens–near the location of the statue of Athena–celebrate a woman whose name is unknown. Philo's Rule 19, "noteworthy omissions," is an understatement here considering she is among the most important participants in the *Project to Preserve.*

The inscriptions identify this woman only as "Juba's Daughter."[120] The ancient Greek geographer Pausanias identifies King Juba II as "Juba the Libyan," and Josephus also refers to him as "Juba, the king of Libya."[121]

One of the inscriptions is dedicated to, "daughter of King Juba,"[122] and the other is in memory of a daughter of a Libyan King.[123]

To earn two inscriptions near the colossal statue of Athena, this daughter of Juba—Antony and Cleopatra's granddaughter—must have done something remarkable. Yet the daughter of Cleopatra Selene and Juba is a mystery no one has been able to satisfactorily solve.

Historians and genealogists agree that she would almost certainly have been named "Cleopatra Thea Philo Pater" after her Grandmother, the Basilissa of Egypt.[124] However, no trace of Juba's daughter or her fate has been found.

Cleopatra and Anthony's daughter Selene was Juba's first wife, and the story of his second wife, examined in excruciating detail in *Following Philo in Search of The*

Magdalene, The Virgin, the Men Called Jesus, deserves a brief recap here:

"In those days a decree went out from Emperor Augustus that all the world should be registered. This was the first census and was taken while Quirinius was governor of Syria" (Luke 1:1-2).

Mother Mary isn't the only virgin thread tied to the Census of Quirinius; Josephus introduces another intriguing virgin in both *Wars* and *Antiquities*. We find her when we return to the Census and are reminded that, "Quirinius had disposed of Archelaus' money...when the census was concluded, which was made in the thirty-seventh year of Caesar's victory over Antony at Actium..."[125]

The reason Augustus Caesar dispatched Quirinius to conduct the census—and to dispose of Archelaus' money—was reported in *Antiquities*.

It is the story of a virgin whose name may be a combination of "Glaucus" (Athena's Owl of Wisdom) and "pyra," Greek for "fire." Her name was "Gla-pyra," suggesting she was a *Vestal* Virgin, women who preserved the perpetual fire of the goddess Vesta, an enigmatic reference to the royal bloodline traced to Sarah.

The Virgin Glaphyra was the daughter of Archelaus, King of Cappadocia, a hotbed of temple prostitution, according to Eusebius.[126] Her mother's name is notably omitted.

Josephus reports that Glaphyra was married, "while she was a virgin,"[127] to Alexander, *the son of King Herod and the Hasmonean princess Mariame*. It should be noted that Antony and Cleopatra also had a son named "Alexander Helios" who was the same age.

King Herod allegedly killed his son, Prince Alexander, c. 7 BCE. Later the widow Glaphyra married Juba the king of Libya, whose first wife was Cleopatra Selene. Josephus reports erroneously that Juba died c. 6 CE,[128] at which time

Prince Alexander's half-brother Archelaus (Herod's son with a non-Jew) divorced his wife, another Mariame. He then married Glaphyra,

> ...who, during her marriage to him, saw the following dream: She thought she saw Alexander ... at which she rejoiced, and embraced him ... but he complained ... "O Glaphyra! You have proved the saying to be true, that saying which assures us that women are not to be trusted. Did you not pledge your faith to me? And were you not married to me when you were a virgin?"[129]

Immediately preceding the story of the Virgin Glaphyra, Josephus tells the story of the "Spurious Alexander" who claimed to be her husband, Herod's Jewish son.[130] This Alexander swore that he and his brother Aristobulus had not been executed as Herod ordered.

However, Augustus Caesar personally judged him to be "spurious" because his hands were rough[131] from the work he did—i.e., carpentry?

When Glaphyra married Juba, their children became step-siblings. And Glaphyra's son Alexander IV and Juba and Cleopatra Selene's eldest daughter were about the same age, both with the royal blood that originated with Sarah.

"Juba's Daughter" is unnamed because she carried more than one name during her lifetime. She is Elabarak Alexander's unknown and unnamed wife (a "noteworthy omission"), mother of sons, possibly twins, Julius and Marcus.

Elabarak Alexander, also known as "Yah-Zeus," "helped make Mary male" – more than once. The first time he did so, he helped make her their sons' "Uncle Philo." She would later become the freedman Pallas, as in "Pallas-Athena."

The goddess Pallas-Athena frequently disguised herself as a man. And it was almost certainly the freedman Pallas who directed the plan to weave the history among a multitude of sources–all of whom were descendants of Julius and Cleopatra.

Pliny the Younger sent tongue-in-cheek letters to his friend Montanus that reveal two important messages.

The first letter describes a monument built to honor Pallas the freedman: "There stands on the road to Tibur, this side of the first milestone — I noticed it quite lately — a monument to Pallas..."[132]

This monument to Pallas is the *Baker's Tomb,* which was buried beneath a massive structure c. 420 when heretical structures throughout the Roman Empire, including the temple of the Vestal Virgins, were being destroyed.

The second letter goes to great lengths to reveal the freedman Pallas' accomplishments and honors while enigmatically disclosing the most heretical secret of all: the most powerful *man* in first century Rome was a *woman—* or rather, *a god without a penis*:

> Gaius Plinius to his friend Montanus: Greetings. As you know from my last letter,[133] I recently saw the monument of Pallas with this inscription: The senate decreed the praetorian ornaments and 15,000,000 HS for this man on account of his extraordinary loyalty and pietas towards his patrons. He was content with the honor.
>
> I then decided that it might be worth the effort to look up the actual decree of the senate. I found it so effusive and verbose that the arrogant inscription seemed moderate and humble by comparison. If all the Africani, Achaici, Numantini – and I will not speak only of the ancient, but even more recent characters such as the Marri, Sullae, and Pompeys (I will not go on any longer) – should they put themselves all together they would still fall short of the praise of Pallas.
>
> Should I think that the people who voted on this were witty or wretched? I would say witty, if wit was appropriate for the senate; I would say wretched, but I have no idea how wretched one would have to be that he could be compelled to say this sort of thing. Maybe it was ambition and a desire

to get ahead. But who could be so insane that he would want to get ahead through his own and the state's disgrace in a state in which the reward for the highest office is to be the first person in the senate to be able to praise Pallas?

I pass over the fact that praetorian ornaments were offered to the slave Pallas (since they were offered by slaves); I pass over the fact that they voted that he should not just be encouraged, but actually compelled to wear a golden ring, for it would lower the dignity of the senate if an ex-praetor wore the iron ring of a slave.

These trivialities may be ignored; what must stand on record is that the senate, on behalf of Pallas – (the senate house has not subsequently been purified) – that the senate gave thanks to Caesar on behalf of Pallas because he spoke about him with the highest honor and gave the senate the chance to testify to their appreciation of him.

What could be more pleasant for the senate than that it should seem to be sufficiently grateful to Pallas? It was added, "That Pallas, to whom all say that they are obliged with the best of their ability, has received the most justly deserved reward for his singular faith and industry." You would think that he had extended the borders of the Empire, or that he had brought the armies of the state home again!

And there follows that, "Since there will be no more gratifying occasion for the Roman senate and people to display their generosity than if it should be able to add to the resources of the most abstemious and faithful manager of the Emperor's wealth." This then was the prayer of the senate; this was the particular joy of the people; this was the most pleasant material for demonstrating liberality: that the fortune of Pallas should be increased by wasting public money.

What next? The senate wished that he be given 15,000,000 HS from the treasury, and since his soul was so far removed for all desires of this sort, the senate should ask all the more fervently that the Father of the state should compel him to accede to the wishes of the senate!

The only thing that was missing was for Pallas to be approached on public authority, for Pallas to be begged to accede to the wishes of the senate, that Caesar himself, the patron of that arrogant abstinence, should make the request in person that he should not spurn 15,000,000 HS!

Pallas did reject it! The only thing he could have done that was more arrogant than to accept so much money from the public treasury was to reject it. The senate took this with further praises, though this time couched with a complaint, in these words: "When the best Emperor and Father of the State was asked by Pallas that the part of the decree of the senate that pertained to giving him 15,000,000 HS from the public treasury be rescinded, the senate states that it bestowed this amount freely and with good reason amongst the other honors that it voted because of Pallas' faith and diligence; and since it felt that it was not right to oppose the will of the Emperor in any manner, he ought to obey him in this manner as well."

Can you imagine Pallas, vetoing, as it were, a decree of the senate, moderating his own honors, refusing 15,000,000 HS as too much, and taking praetorian insignia as being of less importance! Imagine the Emperor obedient to the prayers, or rather, the orders, of his freedman before the senate (for the freedman ordered his patron that he should make this request in the senate)!

Imagine the senate going so far as to assert that it offered this sum, amongst other honors, freely and deservedly to Pallas, and that it would persevere if it did not have to bow to the will of the Emperor, whom it was not right to oppose in any way. So, in order that Pallas not take 15,000,000 HS out of the public treasury, it took his modesty, and the obedience of the senate, which would not have happened in this case, if it had not been thought right to disobey on any point!

You think that this is all? Hold on and hear some more. Since it will be a good thing that the generous promptness of the Emperor to praise and reward deserving people be known everywhere, and especially in those places where those who are entrusted with the management of affairs might be incited to imitation, and where outstanding loyalty and innocence, as exemplified by Pallas should be able to encourage zeal for honest emulation, that those things that the Emperor had said before a full meeting of the senate on January 23, and the decrees of the senate that had been passed in subsequent meeting, should be inscribed on bronze and that the bronze tablet[134] should be erected next to the armored statue of the Divine Julius."

It was not enough for the senate house to be witness to these disgraceful events, but a very public place was chosen in which these events would be published so that they could be read by contemporaries and members of future generations! It was decreed that all the honors of this dutiful slave should be inscribed on bronze, along with those that he had refused, and those that he took up insofar as those voting them had the power to do it. The praetorian ornaments of Pallas were cut and inscribed on a public monument[135] for all time just like ancient treaties, just as if they were sacred laws.[136] So far did the Emperor, so far did the senate, so far did the – I don't know what to call it – of Pallas go that they wished to display the insolence of Pallas, the subservience of Caesar and the humiliation of the senate for all to see! Nor were they ashamed to find a reason for their wretched conduct, a wonderful and beautiful reason, that others would be encouraged by the example of Pallas with enthusiasm for rewards and emulation!

Honors, even those that Pallas did not refuse, were to be cheap. Nevertheless, people of good family could be found who competed for and desired those very honors that they saw given to freedmen and promised to slaves.

How glad I am that I did not live in those days, I would be ashamed if I had. I don't doubt that you feel the same way since I know what a lively and freeborn mind you have; it has been easier for me, even though I have allowed my indignation in places to go beyond the accepted limits of a letter, you will know that I have grieved less rather than too much. Farewell.[137]

How in the world could a woman disguise herself as a man? Her voice would surely give her away. We turn to Tacitus who explains *how* she got away with it:

> ...the proved innocence of Pallas did not please men so much as his arrogance offended them. When his freedmen, his alleged accomplices, were called, they reported that at home Pallas signified his wishes only by a nod or a gesture, or, if further explanation was

required, he used writing, so as not to degrade his voice in such company.[138]

As Claudius' powerful freedmen Narcissus[139] and Pallas, this Divine Duo continued to build on the foundation established by their ancestors. Their ambitious goal was to create Plato's Ideal City, The Golden Age of Rome, and The New Jerusalem.

Baker's Tomb and Porta Maggiore
Rome, Italy
Photo by Gott, June 2023

Chapter Twelve

The Bakers' Tomb

Baker's Tomb, Rome Italy
Photograph by Gott, June, 2015

The Baker's Tomb is a monument constructed next to the Porta Maggiore, Rome's East Gate, a virtual duplicate of Jerusalem's East Gate and the monument Pliny references in his letters to Montanus. The couple whose remains were interred there are identified as *former slaves* who became successful *bakers*, a claim inspired by *Joseph the Nazar and his Mother,* but still unacknowledged by the men in power.

Circa 420, after Paul's Christianity became the official religion of Rome, Emperor Honorius (384–423) ordered workers to bury the *Baker's Tomb,* the *Porta Maggiore,* and the *Neo-Pythagorean Basilica* under a massive stone structure, also called "Porta Maggiore."

Porta Maggiore from c. 420 until 1838[140]

The Baker's Tomb would have been a big part of the annual Crucifixion-Resurrection Festival that honored *The Baker and Her Son.* These celebrations would have carried into the time the destructions began in earnest and the Nazarene sacred structures were buried.

Perhaps more revealing is the decree by Pope Gregory XVI in 1838 that ordered the Baker's Tomb uncovered. This suggests that all the Emperors, Bishops and Popes up to his time must have known the identities of the couple in the buried *House of Bread.*[141]

In 1839, the year after exposing the long-buried tomb of freedmen bakers, Pope Gregory XVI wrote an apostolic letter forbidding the Faithful to participate in the Atlantic Slave Trade. These brief excerpts are worth reading, especially in today's political climate:

> ...we have judged that it belonged to Our pastoral solicitude to exert Ourselves to turn away the Faithful from the inhuman slave trade in Negroes and all other men...desiring to remove such a shame from all the Christian nations...We warn and adjure earnestly in the Lord faithful Christians of every condition that no one in the future dare to...reduce to servitude, or lend aid and favor to those who give themselves up to these practices, or exercise that inhuman traffic by which the Blacks, as if they were not men but rather animals, having been brought into servitude, in no matter what way, are, without any distinction, in contempt of the rights of justice and humanity...

Twenty-two years later, following the election of Abraham Lincoln, Confederate forces determined to preserve slavery attacked Fort Sumter; America's Civil War had begun. How much blame—or credit—belongs to Pope Gregory is anyone's guess. But it seems certain that his efforts were important to the cause of freedom for all, regardless of class or color.

Unfortunately, freedom *for all* is yet to be realized, and a renewed assault on the value of the Feminine is being threatened.

Wikipedia sources date the tomb's construction to c. 50-20 BCE. However, evidence for a later date comes from *The Archaeology of Rome* by John Henry Parker (1806–1884). Parker was an English archaeologist who specialized in ancient architecture, and in 1877, he challenged the dating.

Parker argues that the tomb was built after the aqueducts and after Claudius constructed Rome's East Gate, the *Porta Maggiore*, which identifies Rome as "The New Jerusalem" (52 CE).[142]

Additional artifacts discovered near the tomb provide clues to the identities of the interred couple. Parker notes:

> A very early date was at first assigned to it, and Canina is disposed to think it of the time of the Republic, but it must be near the end of it; the construction is evidently of later character than some of the aqueducts. The material is travertine and tufa, the sculpture also is too good for the early part of the Republic. The very singular plan, wider at one end than the other, is accounted for by the situation between two roads converging at the double gate, and these roads are not likely to have been brought so near together before the gate was made.
>
> The tomb was much mutilated, and the second inscription had to be collected from fragments, and amongst them was a sculpture in bas-relief of the baker Eurysacis[143] and his wife Atistia.[144]

Marble Relief of Eurysacis and Atistia[145]

The name, *Eury sacis* is translated "wide small," an apt description of the gates of Claudius' Porta Maggiore pictured below with the Baker's Tomb.

Photograph by P.J. Gott, Rome, June, 2015

Eury and *sacis* could have been chosen to refute any attempt to date the tomb prior to the Porta Maggiore's construction that features *wide* and *narrow* gates.

Clues to the identities of *Eurysacis* and *Atistia* can be teased from inscriptions written in Latin:

EST HOC MONIMENTVM
MARCEI VERGILEI EVRYSACIS
PISTORIS REDEMPTORIS APPARET

Photograph by P.J. Gott, June 2023

Note the three oversized "T," one in each word, that resembles the *Roman Tau Crucifix*. These words are generally translated, "baker, contractor, public servant." However, this translation is acknowledged to be problematic:

APPARET is erroneously translated as a noun ("public servant"); *apparet* is a verb that means "...to come in sight, to appear..."[146] Therefore, the intended translation is more likely, "appeared."

REDEMPTORIS is translated "contractor," but another valid word is "redeemed," as *Goddess the Mother* was redeemed.

PISTORIS, "Baker," refers to Joseph's Mother, the first crucifixion in the Bible and the Goddess who disguised herself as a male.

A better translation:

BAKER REDEEMED APPEARED

This might have been reason enough for Honorius to bury the Baker's Tomb, but the inscribed names also carry clues that expose the deception and restore the truth about Jesus and his Mother:

MARCEI refers to the god Mars, the father of twins Romulus and Remus, mythological founders of Rome; their mother, Rhea Silvia, was a Vestal Virgin.[147] Emperor Tiberius was the paternal grandfather of twin boys whose maternal grandmother was Antonia, Marc Antony's daughter.[148]

VERGILEI refers to Vestal Virgins, the preeminent bakers in the Roman Empire. Vestals led the annual New Year rites on March 1 when new laurel branches replaced the old branches as they relit the sacred fire to symbolize a fresh start of the New Year.[149] The epitaph found with the bas-relief portrait is written in Latin:

FVIT ATISTIA VXOR MIHEI
Atistia was my wife
FEMINA OPITVMA VEIXSIT
A most excellent lady in life
QVOIVS CORPORIS RELIQVIAE
the surviving remains of her body
QUOD SVPERANT SVNT IN
which are in
HOC PANARIO
this breadbasket[150]

Note again the oversized "T" in the words FVIT ("was") and the first "T" in *ATIS TIA*. Note also the slight space between *ATIS* and *TIA*, names of deities popular in the Roman Empire when the tomb was constructed.

Attis was the god without a penis or a goddess disguised as a god; *Tia*, in *Atis-tia*, refers to *Theia* (also *Thia*; *Thea*), the Greek Goddess of Light. Her brother/consort is Hyperion, god of the sun. They are the parents of Helios ("Sun"), Selene ("Moon"), and Eos ("Dawn"). [151]

Cleopatra *Thea Philo* Pater named her twins with Marcus Antonius "Alexander Helios" and "Cleopatra Selene." Selene's daughter with Juba II of Mauretania disappeared from history shortly after she was born, along with her stepbrother, Alexander, King Herod and Mariame's grandson.

Epilogue

Paulus was raised by his uncle Germanicus/Gamaliel and taught the earliest version of Philo's Method. After he abandoned the Nazarenes, he would have shared it with his subordinates and descendants who disparaged it as a dangerous, satanic heresy.

Fortunately, his younger son, Josephus the Jewish historian, chose to join Vespasian to put down his father's revolt and stay in the good graces of the Emperor's family.

Josephus coordinated with the gospel writer Luke to reveal some of the participants in the project to restore respect for the Feminine, enigmatically, of course.

The web of families and names is vast and challenging, perhaps too challenging for aging scholars whose life's work is too sacred to discard and whose remaining time is too short to start anew.

It is a massive project that will require young, thick-skinned, dedicated seekers of the factual history waiting to be pulled from the ashes of imposed ignorance. Parallel events and analogous elements and people tie the Hasmoneans, the Ptolemies, the Julio-Claudians and other dynasties together to weave a far different history than previously known.

Perhaps the fruits collected and shared might nourish the masses with the love and compassion that a resurrected Goddess and Her Son tried to deliver two millennia ago. Or will it be pushed underground another two thousand years?

AI will probably be of immense help.

Hala Ela El!

Polycarp, translated "Many Fruits," is the preserver of YaH-Zeus the Nazarene and an expert practitioner of Philo's Method. He may have also been known as Gaius Suetonius Tranquillus. Whatever his name might have been, this Nazarene gave his life to expose Paul's fraud and to guide *The Way* to *The Historical Jesus*.

Polycarp
Bishop of Smyrna[152]

Appendix A
Approximate Timeline
People and Events

110-18 BCE: Birth/Death of Julius Caesar; Hillel the Elder; King Asander.

64-12 BCE: Birth/Death of Marcus Antonius; Herod the Great; Marcus Agrippa (author of Mark's Hebrew script).

69 BCE-8 CE: Birth/Death of Cleopatra; Mariame; Dynamis.

47 BCE: Birth of Emperor Tiberius, aka, Caesarion, et. al.

15 BCE-74 CE: Birth/Death of Germanicus; Gamaliel; Jesus.

10 BCE-74 CE: Birth/Death of "Juba's Daughter," aka, Agrippina I; Philo; Freedman Pallas; Mary Magdalene.

6 CE-80 CE: Birth/Death of Matthais; Lucius Paulus; Caligula; Apostle Paul (author of Matthew's Gospel).

30 BCE-12 BCE: *Hebrew Marcus* is composed to be performed on the streets of Jerusalem.

37 CE: Ides of March, "alleged death" of Emperor Tiberius.

37-41 CE: Gaius Caligula is Emperor of Rome.

41 CE: Caligula/Paulus imprisons his uncle and threatens to have him executed (*Act's* story of Stephen); Caligula "assassinated" and dethroned.

42 CE: Joseph's Triumph Cameo commissioned to honor Germanicus and Agrippina and to humiliate Paulus.

45-62: Paul's letters to the churches, the beginning of his retribution to that Jezebel bitch Empress!

64-5: High Priest Matthais/Paulus writes the *Gospel of Matthew* and translates and interpolates Hebrew Mark.

75-80: Josephus and Luke Plutarchus coordinate stories of events and people and wrap them in enigmas.

120-130: Suetonius and Tacitus wrap the Julio-Claudian Dynasty in enigmas.

120-140: Polycarp compiles and edits the Christian Bible, composes and adds *Acts* and *the Son of Man Sayings*.

Appendix B
Philo's Rules for Identifying and Solving Enigmas

1. The doubling of a phrase.
2. An apparently superfluous expression in the text.
3. The repetition of statements previously made.
4. A change of phraseology – all these phenomena point to something special that the reader must consider.
5. An entirely different meaning may also be found by disregarding the ordinarily accepted division of the sentence into phrases and clauses and by considering a different combination of the words.
6. Synonyms [and phonetically similar words] must be carefully studied.
7. A play upon words must be utilized for finding a deeper meaning.
8. A definite, allegorical [enigmatical] sense may be gathered from certain particles, adverbs, prepositions, [unclear pronoun antecedents], etc., and in certain cases it can be gathered even from
9. the part of a word.
10. Every word must be explained in *all its meanings* in order that different interpretations may be found.
11. The skillful interpreter may make slight changes in a word, following the rabbinical rule: "Read not so, but so." Philo, therefore, changed accents, breathings, etc., in Hebrew words.
12. Any peculiarity in a phrase justifies the assumption that some special meaning is intended. Details regarding the form of words are very important.

13. Consider the number of the word, if it shows any peculiarity in the singular or the plural: the tense of the verb, etc.
14. The gender of the noun may carry a clue.
15. Note the presence or omission of the article;
16. the artificial interpretation of a single expression;
17. the position of the verses of a passage;
18. peculiar verse combinations;
19. noteworthy omissions;
20. striking statements [i.e., angel, spirit, Holy Spirit, omen, prophecy, etc.];
21. numeral symbolism [i.e., Platonic; Gematria].

---

[1] Charles W. Hedrick, "Unlocking the Secrets of the Gospel According to Thomas," and many others.

[2] David Trobisch, "Paul's Letter Collection: Tracing the Origins," and many others.

[3] Hahn, Scott, ed. (2009). Catholic Bible dictionary (1st ed.). New York: Doubleday. ISBN 978-0-385-51229-9.

[4] Soulen, Richard N.; Soulen, R. Kendall (2001). Handbook of biblical criticism (3rd ed., rev. and expanded. ed.). Louisville, Ky.: Westminster John Knox Press. p. 78. ISBN 0-664-22314-1.

[5] Sinai, Nicolai (2017). The Qur'an: a historical-critical introduction. The new Edinburgh Islamic surveys. Edinburgh: Edinburgh University Press. pp. 2–5. ISBN 978-0-7486-9576-8.

[6] Law, David R. (2012). *The Historical-Critical Method: A Guide for the Perplexed.* T&T Clark. ISBN 978-0-567-40012-3. p. 10–14.

[7] Epiphanius, Panarion 1:19. Emphasis added. (*The Panarion of Epiphanius of Salamis: A treatise Against Eighty Sects in Three Books*.) Masselana: http://www.masseiana.org/panarion_bk1.htm

[8] Asherah, Strong's Hebrew 842, Biblehub: https://biblehub.com/hebrew/842.htm

[9] Ahab, Strong's Hebrew 256, Biblehub: https://biblehub.com/hebrew/256.htm

[10] *Ba'eL* can also be rendered *aB eL* and translated, "Father God." "Asherah" and "Father God" are *Elohim*, correctly translated "Gods."

[11] "[Jez-aba'el's] actions and influence were in direct opposition to the covenantal faith of Israel, which demanded exclusive worship of

Yahweh. Jezebel's account is set during the 9th century BCE, a time of political turmoil and religious syncretism in the Northern Kingdom of Israel." The name "Jezreel" means "God sows" or "God will scatter (Strong's Hebrew 3157); therefore, Jez-ab'el means "Father El sows/scatters." Jezreel: Biblehub, Strong's Hebrew 3157: https://biblehub.com/hebrew/3157.htm

[12] "Neo-Pythagorean Basilica of Porta Maggiore," ROMA: https://www.turismoroma.it/en/places/neo-pythagorean-basilica-porta-maggiore

[13] Iamblichus' Life of Pythagoras: www.gutenberg.org/files/63300/63300-h/63300-h.htm

[14] Ibid.

[15] Clement, Stromata (1.15): Clement of Alexandria. (ca. 182-201 CE), Stromata: Early Christian Writings (2001-2015): http://www.earlychristianwritings.com/text/clement-stromata-book1.html

[16] C.D. Yonge, trans. The Works of Philo: Complete and Unabridged, "On Dreams." (Peabody: Hendrickson Publishers, 2013), (34.205), 383-4.

[17] Yonge (2013): Philo, "Every Good Man is Free (12.82), 690. Emphasis added.

[18] Plutarch, *Moralia*: "Isis and Osiris," 1st-2nd Century (Introduction).

[19] Irenaeus, "Against Heresies," Alexander Roberts, ed., The Gnostic Society Library Online (1995), 1.9.5.

[20] F. W. Farrar, History of Interpretation: Eight Lectures (London: MacMillan and Co., 1886), 149.

[21] "Philo Judaeus; Attitude toward Literal Meaning," Jewish Encyclopedia Online (1906):
https://jewishencyclopedia.com/articles/12116-philo-judaeus#anchor10

[22] "Philo Judaeus; Attitude toward Literal Meaning," Jewish Encyclopedia Online (1906):
https://jewishencyclopedia.com/articles/12116-philo-judaeus#anchor10

[23] Babylonian Talmud: "...a commentary on the Mishnah, primarily written in Jewish Babylonian Aramaic. It contains the teachings and opinions of thousands of rabbis on a variety of subjects...compiled in the 5th century by Rav Ashi and Ravina II." Wikipedia: "Talmud": https://en.wikipedia.org/wiki/Talmud

[24] The William Davidson Talmud, Sefaria: a Living Library of Jewish Texts Online:
Sanhedrin 88b (7):
https://www.sefaria.org/Sanhedrin.88b.7?lang=bi&with=all&lang2=en

[25] The Jerusalem Talmud, aka, Palestinian Talmud: "Prior to being written down, it was transmitted orally for centuries and represents a compilation of scholastic teachings and analyses on the Mishnah (especially those concerning agricultural laws) found across regional centres of the Land of Israel now known as the Academies in Galilee (principally those of Tiberias, Sepphoris, and Caesarea). It is written largely in Jewish Palestinian Aramaic, a Western Aramaic language that differs from its Babylonian counterpart." Wikipedia: "Talmud": https://en.wikipedia.org/wiki/Talmud

[26] "Hypatia, Mathematician and astronomer," Michael Deakin; Britannica: "She was, in her time, the world's leading mathematician and astronomer, the only woman for whom such claim can be made. She was also a popular teacher and lecturer on philosophical topics… Her philosophy was Neoplatonist and was thus seen as "pagan" at a time of bitter religious conflict between Christians (both orthodox and "heretical"), Jews, and pagans. Her Neoplatonism was concerned with the approach to the One, an underlying reality partially accessible via the human power of abstraction from the Platonic forms, themselves abstractions from the world of everyday reality. Her philosophy also led her to embrace a life of dedicated virginity.". https://www.britannica.com/biography/Hypatia

[27] Southwood, Katherine E: "Bible Odyssey," article, "Intermarriage in Ezra-Nehemiah," https://www.bibleodyssey.org/articles/intermarriage-in-ezra-nehemiah/

[28] This "key" is still available if modern "rules" for translating Biblical Hebrew that prohibit the interpretational freedoms enjoyed at the time of Jesus are ignored.

[29] Torah: Genesis, Exodus, Leviticus, Numbers and Deuteronomy. Tanakh is an acronym, made from the first Hebrew letter of each of the Masoretic Text's three traditional divisions: Torah (literally 'Instruction' or 'Law'), Nevi'im (Prophets), and Ketuvim (Writings)—hence TaNaKh.

[30] "Houses of Hillel and Shammai," Wikipedia, https://en.wikipedia.org/wiki/Houses_of_Hillel_and_Shammai

[31] *shama*, Strong's Hebrew 8035, Biblehub: https://biblehub.com/hebrew/8085.htm

[32] *Yahweh Shammah*, Strong's Hebrew 3074, Biblehub: https://biblehub.com/hebrew/3074.htm

[33] "Yawist," Encyclopedia.com, https://www.encyclopedia.com/philosophy-and-religion/judaism/judaism/yahwist

[34] "Hillel the Elder," Wikipedia, https://en.wikipedia.org/wiki/Hillel_the_Elder

[35] "Hillel," Jewish Encyclopedia online:
https://www.jewishencyclopedia.com/articles/7698-hillel
[36] ZUGOT (lit. "pairs"); by: Joseph Jacobs, Jacob Zallel Lauterbach. Jewish Encyclopedia,
https://www.jewishencyclopedia.com/articles/15293-zugot
[37] Menahem the Essene was "…a Jewish tanna sage living during the era of the Zugot (lit. "pairs"). As such, he was 'paired' with Hillel the Elder and served as *Av Beit Din*."
Wikipedia: "Menahem the Essene:
https://en.wikipedia.org/wiki/Menahem_the_Essene
[38] Jewish Encyclopedia online, "Hillel," Section heading "The Golden Rule" (Shabbat 31(a).
[39] Jewish Virtual Library, "Hillel and Shammai";
https://www.jewishvirtuallibrary.org/hillel-and-shammai#google_vignette
[40] Josephus, 1999, *Antiquities* 20.9.4 (213-214), 657. "And now Jesus, the son of Gamaliel, became the successor of Jesus, the son of Damneus, in the high priesthood…"
[41] Jewish Encyclopedia, "Gamaliel I," Schechter, Solomon; Bacher, Wilhelm.
[42] Strong's Hebrew 853: "Not typically translated; used as a direct object marker," Biblehub: https://biblehub.com/hebrew/853.htm
[43] "David Trobisch," German scholar whose work has focused on formation of the Christian Bible, ancient New Testament manuscripts and the epistles of Paul. Wikipedia,
https://en.wikipedia.org/wiki/David_Trobisch
[44] Trobisch, D. (2007/2008, December-January). "Who Published the New Testament?". New Inquiry, pp. 30-33.
[45] "Polycarp – Martyrdom," Polycarp.net. "Polycarp," Wikipedia (Polycarp, 2021):
[46] *Stephen*, Strong's Greek 4736, Biblehub:
https://biblehub.com/greek/4736.htm
[47] *nezer*, Strong's Hebrew 5145, Biblehub:
https://biblehub.com/hebrew/5145.htm
[48] *nazar*, Strong's Hebrew 5144, Biblehub:
https://biblehub.com/hebrew/5144.htm
[49] *nazir*, Strong's Hebrew 5139, Biblehub:
https://biblehub.com/hebrew/5139.htm
[50] Also written *Alabarch*.
[51] Philo of Alexandria, *On the Embassy to Gaius*, Early Christian Writings, The Works of Philo:
https://www.earlychristianwritings.com/yonge/book40.html

[52] Josephus, 1999, *Antiquities* 19.5.1 (276), 633.
[53] *eL*: Strong's Hebrew 413, Biblehub: https://biblehub.com/hebrew/413.htm
[54] *Lo*: Strong's Hebrew 3808, Biblehub: https://biblehub.com/hebrew/3808.htm
[55] *aL*: Strong's Hebrew 409, Biblehub: https://biblehub.com/hebrew/409.htm
[56] *shadday*, Strong's Hebrew 7706, Biblehub: https://biblehub.com/hebrew/7706.htm
[57] *shad*, Strong's Hebrew 7699, Biblehub: https://biblehub.com/hebrew/7699.htm
[58] Philo's Rule 14: "The gender of the noun may carry a clue"; "glory" is Greek, doxa, Strong's Greek 1391, a feminine noun.
[59] Nazir, Strong's Hebrew 5139; Biblehub: https://biblehub.com/hebrew/5139.htm
[60] Hebrew LHMLLHM.
[61] Jacob is renamed "Israel," from Isha oRa eL, "Woman light God."
[62] "Kisar" was the Sumerian-Babylonian "first mother." Ki means "Earth," Sar means "princess." Kisar is the etymology of Rome's "Caesar" and Germany's "Kaisar."
[63] meseq, Strong's Hebrew 4943, defined as "acquisition, possession, heir"; trans. "steward." Biblehub: https://biblehub.com/hebrew/meshek_4943.htm
[64] "Sanctuary of Attis," https://www.ostia-antica.org/regio4/1/1-3.htm; Photo by Klaus Heese, cropped. The original is in the Vatican Museums.
[65] Gospel of Thomas, Saying 114.
[66] *The Birth of the Synoptics* (Michael J. Wrenn, trans.; Chicago: Franciscan Herald Press, 1987), p1.
[67] "Kishar," Wikipedia: https://en.wikipedia.org/wiki/Kishar
[68] Nicolaus of Damascus' account appears in Workman, B.K. "They Saw it Happen in Classical Times" (1964);.
[69] Etsy: https://www.etsy.com/listing/753248767/?ga_order=most_relevant&cns=1
[70] Duane W. Roller, The World of Juba II and Kleopatra Selene; (New York and London: Routledge Taylor & Frances Group, 2003), 55-7. "Nicolaus of Damascus," Wikipedia: https://en.wikipedia.org/wiki/Nicolaus_of_Damascus
[71] Translated, "mighty power." Asander's wife Dynamis left inscriptions referring to August Caesar as "Theos" and "son of Theos." Luke's Gospel identifies Dynamis as the "angel" who prophesies that "Dio … will be holy; he will be called 'Son of Theos.'"

[72] Workman, B.K. (1964), "They Saw it Happen in Classical Times." Internet Archive Books:
https://archive.org/details/theysawithappeni0000bkwo_g5v5
[73] Workman, B.K. (1964)
[74] Ibid.
[75] "Lamed Vav Zaddikim," Jewish Virtual Library Online:
https://www.jewishvirtuallibrary.org/lamed-vav-x1e92-addikim
[76] Zwerin, Rabbi Raymond A. (September 15, 2002). "The 36 - Who Are They?": Temple Sinai, Denver: americanet.com.
[77] The Talmud ties *Shechina* to Nasi Gamaliel, also known as "Jesus the Nazarene": (Abulafia, 1170-1244. *Babylonian Talmud*, Sanhedrin Folio 39a).
[78] NAS (Strong's Hebrew 5144b), *nazar*, as in "Nazarite" and "Nazarene."
[79] Zwerin, Rabbi Raymond A. (September 15, 2002). "The 36 - Who Are They?": Temple Sinai, Denver: americanet.com..
[80] "Tsadikim Nistarim," Wikipedia:
https://en.wikipedia.org/wiki/Tzadikim_Nistarim
[81] Plutarch, *Life of Julius Caesar* (Loeb, 1919), (Thayer Online 66.1).
[82] "Dynamis (queen)," Wikipedia:
https://en.wikipedia.org/wiki/Dynamis_(queen)
"Asander (king)," Wikipedia:
https://en.wikipedia.org/wiki/Asander_(king)
"Aspurgus," Wikipedia: https://en.wikipedia.org/wiki/Aspurgus
[83] Image from: Classical Numismatic Group, Inc. CC BY-SA 3.0. File: S0484.4.jpg. Uploaded by Carlomorino, January 25, 2006.
[84] S.T. Davis, D. Kendall, G. O'Collins. *The Trinity*. (Oxford: Oxford University Press, 2002), 30. (N.V.) Also, "Dynamis Bosporan Queen," Wikipedia (Dynamis (Bosporan queen), 2017).
[85] "The Pyramid of Caius Cestius": ROMA, Live Rome, Discover Rome: https://www.turismoroma.it/en/places/pyramid-caius-cestius
[86] Suetonius, *Life of Julius Caesar* (Loeb, 1914), (Thayer Online 88.1).
[87] Duane W. Roller, *The World of Juba II and Kleopatra Selene*; (New York and London: Routledge Taylor & Frances Group, 2003), 55-7. Emphasis added.
Roller's observations are supported by Wikipedia sources in the article, "Nicolaus of Damascus," Wikipedia:
https://en.wikipedia.org/wiki/Nicolaus_of_Damascus
[88] Cleopatra was known as the *New Isis*, Plutarch, *Life of Antony* (Loeb, 1920), (Thayer Online 54.6); Antony was hailed as, *Dionysus Carnivorous*, Plutarch, *Life of Antony* (Loeb, 1920), (Thayer Online 24.3).

[89] Plutarch, *Life of Antony* (Loeb, 1920), (Thayer Online 86.1-2).
[90] K.A. Morrow, Disputation in Stone: Jews Imagined on the Saint Stephen Portal of Paris Cathedral, in M. Merback (ed.), Beyond the Yellow Badge: Anti-Judaism and Antisemitism in Medieval and Early Modern Visual Culture, Leiden, 2007, p. 81. See also: M. Avisseau-Broustet, Le Grand Camée de la Sainte-Chapelle, in J. Durand - M.-P. Laffitte (edd.), Le Trésor de la Sainte-Chapelle, Parijs, 2001, pp. 90-95 (non vidi).
[91] E. Zwierlein-Diehl, Antike Gemmen und ihr Nachleben, Berlin, 2007, p. 245
[92] Ibid.
[93] i.e., The *Metamorphoses*, by Ovid, Project Gutenberg: https://www.gutenberg.org/files/21765/21765-h/21765-h.htm
[94] *The Lives of the Twelve Caesars: The Life of Julius Caesar*; English translation Rolfe, J. C., *Suetonius, The Lives of the Twelve Caesars* (London, 1913-14, Section 61): https://droitromain.univ-grenoble-alpes.fr/Anglica/Suetonius1_engl.gr.htm
"He rode a remarkable horse, too, with feet that were almost human; for its hoofs were cloven in such a way as to look like toes. This horse was foaled on his own place, and since the soothsayers had declared that it foretold the rule of the world for its master, he reared it with the greatest care, and was the first to mount it, for it would endure no other rider. Afterwards, too, he dedicated a statue of it before the temple of Venus Genetrix.
[95] "Augustus and Imperial Cult," Ebrary: https://ebrary.net/140782/history/augustus_imperial_cult
[96] "Tiberius Claudius Narcissus," Wikipedia: https://en.wikipedia.org/wiki/Tiberius_Claudius_Narcissus
[97] "Marcus Antonius Pallas," Wikipedia: https://en.wikipedia.org/wiki/Pallas_(freedman)
[98] Gospel of Thomas, Saying 114: "Simon Peter said... 'Let's put Mary out of our group, for women are not worthy of life.' Jesus replied, '...*I myself will lead her to make her male,* so that even she may become a live spirit...'"
[99] Gospel of Thomas, Saying 114: perhaps the term "live spirit" means "remembered forever."
[100] Greek word, *leitourgeó*, is defined as "To minister, to serve, **to perform a public duty**": https://biblehub.com/greek/3008.htm. Suetonius reports: "Being once called "Lord," [Emperor Tiberius] warned the speaker not to address him again in an insulting fashion."

Suetonius, *The Lives of the Twelve Caesars: The Life of Tiberius* (J. C. Rolfe, London, 1913-14) #27.

[101] Niger, Strong's Greek 3526, "Latin origin meaning black." Biblehub: https://biblehub.com/greek/3526.htm

[102] Acts 9:1-19; Acts 22:6-16; Acts 26:12-18.

[103] 2 Cor 12:1-10.

[104] Suetonius, *Life of Vespasian* (Loeb, 1914), (Thayer Online 4.1).

[105] Ben Witherington III, *The Acts of the Apostles: A Socio-Rhetorical Commentary,* 399-400. Witherington, 1998. Rome Inscription: GIL VI.3 1545.

[106] Latin Word Study Tool: Perseus Digital Library: https://www.perseus.tufts.edu/hopper//morph?l=servare&la=la

[107] "Julia the Younger," Wikipedia: https://en.wikipedia.org/wiki/Julia_the_Younger

[108] Ibid.

[109] Ibid.

[110] "Marcus Aemilius Lepidus (executed by Caligula," Wikipedia: https://en.wikipedia.org/wiki/Marcus_Aemilius_Lepidus_(executed_by _Caligula) Emphasis added.

[111] "Caligula," Wikipedia: https://en.wikipedia.org/wiki/Caligula

[112] Ibid.

[113] Suetonius, *Life of Caligula* (Loeb, 1914), (Thayer Online 8.1-5).

[114] Emphasis added.

[115] Alexander Kazhdan, ed. (1991), Oxford Dictionary of Byzantium, Oxford University Press, 264.

[116] Suetonius reports that Gaius Caligula was born... "when his father was consul." Germanicus was consul in 12 CE; however, Lucius Aemilius Paulus, Julia the Younger's husband and father of her eldest son born in 6, was consul in 6. Suetonius, *Life of Caligula* (Loeb, 1914), (Thayer Online 8.1-5).

[117] Suetonius, Life of Augustus, 19; "Lucius Aemilius Paullus," Wikipedia: https://en.wikipedia.org/wiki/Lucius_Aemilius_Paullus_(consul_1)#cite _note-5

[118] "The gesture dates back to ancient Greece and it was also used in ancient Rome"; "The Finger": Wikipedia: https://en.wikipedia.org/wiki/The_finger

[119] "High Priests of the Second Temple Period, Jewish Virtual Library: https://www.jewishvirtuallibrary.org/high-priests-of-the-second-temple-period

[120] "Cleopatra of Mauretania," Hellenica World: https://www.hellenicaworld.com/Greece/Person/en/CleopatraOfMauretania.html
[121] Josephus, 1999, *Antiquities* 17.13.4 (349), 584.
[122] Athenian inscription, IG II 3439.
[123] Athenian inscription *IG* III 1309.
[124] Chris Bennett: Genealogy of Cleopatra Selene (2001).
[125] Josephus, 1999, *Antiquities* 18.2.1 (26), 588. This calculates to 6 CE.
[126] Eusebius, *Life of Constantine*, 3.55 and 3.58.
[127] Josephus, 1999, *Antiquities* 17.13.4 (349), 584.
[128] Josephus, 1999, *Antiquities* 17.13.4 (350), 584.
[129] Josephus, 1999, *Antiquities* 17.13.4 (349-351), 584.
[130] Josephus, 1999, *Antiquities* 17.12.1-2 (324-338), 582-3.
[131] Josephus, 1999, *Antiquities* 17.12.2 (333), 583.
[132] 151   Full text of "The letters of the younger Pliny; literally translated by John Delaware Lewis"; (Loeb, VII. 29)
[133] The referenced letter (Loeb, VII. 29) also quotes the inscription on "the monument" and places this monument to a freedman on the east side of Rome.
[134] In addition to a "monument," a "bronze tablet" with inscriptions.
[135] Again, Pliny refers to a "monument for all time" with inscriptions.
[136] Possibly a reference to the inscriptions in Athens honoring Juba's daughter.
[137] Pliny the Younger, *The Letters of Pliny the Consul with Occasional Remarks*, William Melmoth, Esq, ed. (Edinburgh: 1807) 2.8.6 (85). Emphasis added.
[138] Tacitus, *Annals; The Works* (1864-1877), (Sacred Texts Online 13.23).
[139] The Gnostics' "Secret Book of John" alludes to *Narcissus* just before "the image of the Perfect and Invisible Virgin Spirit," appears. She is called "Barbelo," *BaR aB eL* and/or *aB oR aB eL*. See Meyer, 2008, 110. "The Secret Book of John," *The Nag Hammadi Scriptures*, footnote 13: "The Father gazes into the water and falls in love with his own image in a manner that calls to mind Narcissus in Greek mythology (see Ovid *Metamorphoses* 3.402-510)."
[140] Vasi Plate #7, Rome Art Lover: https://www.romeartlover.it/Vasi07.html
[141] Hebrew, *BeTh LeHeM*; Strong's Hebrew 1035; Biblehub: https://biblehub.com/hebrew/1035.htm
[142] "Porta Maggiore," Wikipedia: https://en.wikipedia.org/wiki/Porta_Maggiore
[143] Correction: "The Baker" was not Eurysacis but his wife, Atis-tia.

[144] John Henry Parker, *The Archaeology of Rome, Part IX*, "Tombs in and Near Rome" (Oxford: James Parker and Co; London: John Murray, Albemarle Street, 1877), 34-5. Public Domain.
[145] "Restored baker and his wife back on display": The History Blog: https://www.thehistoryblog.com/archives/54452
[146] Perseus Digital Library, Gregory R. Crain, Editor in Chief, Tufts University. Latin Word Study Tool, online.
[147] "Romulus and Remus," Wikipedia.
[148] "Tiberius Gemellus," Wikipedia: https://en.wikipedia.org/wiki/Tiberius_Gemellus
[149] Wildfang, 2006, 1-31.
[150] Image: Jastrow (2006) Public Domain. Current location: Baths of Diocletian. Corpus inscriptorum latinarum, 1.2, 1206.
[151] "Theia": Wikipedia: https://en.wikipedia.org/wiki/Theia
[152] Image downloaded from: https://orthodoxwiki.org/images/4/41/Polycarp.jpg

www.ingramcontent.com/pod-product-compliance
Lightning Source LLC
Chambersburg PA
CBHW071731040426
42446CB00011B/2306